BOISE

TRAVEL GUIDE

2024

Boise Getaway: Practical Tips and Resources for Every Traveler.

BY

TILDA ROMERO

Copyright © 2024 TILDA ROMERO.

All Rights Reserved.

Table of Contents

Disclaimer 5

Introduction 7

    Discover Boise: A City of Vibrant Culture and Outdoor Adventure 9

Chapter 1: Exploring Boise's Urban Charms 13

    Downtown Boise: Historic Landmarks and Modern Delights 13

    Boise River Greenbelt: A Serene Escape in the Heart of the City 17

    Basque Block: A Cultural Journey through Boise's Basque Heritage 20

Chapter 2: Outdoor Escapes 25

    Boise Foothills: Hiking Trails and Panoramic Views 25

    Bogus Basin: Year-Round Mountain Adventure 28

    Julia Davis Park: Green Oasis with Museums and Attractions 32

Chapter 3: Cultural Delights 37

    Idaho State Capitol: Iconic Architecture and History 37

    Boise Art Museum: Contemporary Art and Exhibitions ... 41

Idaho Botanical Garden: Blooms and Beauty in Every Season 45

Chapter 4: Dining and Local Flavors.......................................51

Boise's Best Eateries: From Farm-to-Table to Global Cuisine 51

North End District: Quaint Cafes and Neighborhood Charm...55

Boise Brewing: Craft Beer and Local Brews to Savor 60

Chapter 5: Day Trips and Beyond 65

Snake River Valley Wine Region: Wine Tastings and Scenic Drives..65

Sun Valley Resort: Skiing, Golf, and Year-Round Recreation..69

Shoshone Falls: The "Niagara of the West" in Twin Falls 74

Chapter 6: Events and Festivals 79

Treefort Music Fest: Indie Music and Community Vibes.79

Boise River Festival: Waterfront Celebrations and Family Fun 83

Boise Farmers Market: Fresh Produce and Local Goods Galore 88

Chapter 7: Insider Tips and Recommendations....................93

Local Favorites: Hidden Gems and Must-Try Experiences 93

Budget-Friendly Boise: Free and Low-Cost Activities 103

Planning Your Visit: Practical Tips for a Seamless Trip .109

Useful Contacts and Resources 119

Conclusion..127

Disclaimer

Dear Reader,

Thank you for choosing our Boise Travel Guide as your companion to exploring Idaho's capital city. We have crafted this guide with meticulous care, aiming to provide you with comprehensive information, insider tips, and valuable resources to enhance your Boise experience.

However, you may have noticed that this guide does not include images. Here are the reasons why:

Focus on Detailed Information: Our priority was to deliver detailed descriptions, practical addresses, and insightful recommendations that help you navigate Boise effectively. By focusing on text rather than images, we aimed to provide a more thorough exploration of the city's attractions, dining options, and local resources.

Reader's Imagination: We believe in stimulating your imagination and curiosity about Boise's landmarks, neighborhoods, and natural beauty through vivid descriptions and engaging narratives. This approach allows you to envision yourself strolling through Boise's streets, enjoying its parks, and discovering its hidden gems.

Practicality and Portability: By omitting images, we aimed to keep this guide practical and portable, making it easy for you to carry and reference during your travels. This format ensures that you have quick access to essential information without the bulk of additional visual content.

We understand that visual imagery can enhance the reader's experience, and we encourage you to supplement this guide with online resources, local maps, and personal photography to capture Boise's captivating scenery and vibrant atmosphere.

Once again, thank you for choosing our Boise Travel Guide. We hope it serves as a valuable companion on your journey through Boise, helping you uncover its charm, culture, and endless possibilities for exploration.

Happy travels!

Introduction

Welcome to Boise, where urban sophistication meets outdoor adventure in the heart of Idaho. Nestled against the backdrop of the majestic Rocky Mountains and cradled by the serene Boise River, this vibrant city offers a tapestry of experiences waiting to be explored. Whether you're drawn to historic landmarks, cultural festivals, or the boundless beauty of nature, Boise promises a journey that will captivate and inspire.

Boise is more than just a city; it's a community rich in heritage and creativity. From its bustling downtown, adorned with unique shops and cafes, to the expansive Boise River Greenbelt, where cyclists and walkers weave through a verdant oasis, every corner of Boise invites discovery. Dive into the city's Basque Block, where echoes of European culture resonate through traditional festivals and cuisine, or hike the Boise Foothills for panoramic views that stretch to the horizon.

Art enthusiasts will find solace in Boise's cultural offerings, from the renowned Boise Art Museum showcasing contemporary works to the tranquil Idaho Botanical Garden, where flora blooms in harmony with sculptures and winding paths. History buffs can explore the Idaho State Capitol, a symbol of the city's enduring spirit, while foodies can indulge in farm-to-table delights in the North End or savor local brews at Boise Brewing.

Throughout the year, Boise comes alive with events that celebrate its diverse spirit. From the eclectic Treefort Music Fest that pulses with indie beats across venues, to the Boise River Festival where families gather along the waterfront for games and festivities, the city's calendar is dotted with experiences that unite locals and visitors alike.

Whether you're planning a weekend getaway or a longer stay, this guide is your gateway to Boise's hidden gems and must-see attractions. Join us as we uncover the essence of Boise—a city that welcomes you with open arms and promises an unforgettable journey through its landscapes, culture, and community.

Discover Boise: A City of Vibrant Culture and Outdoor Adventure

Downtown Boise: Where History Meets Modern Charm

Boise's downtown area is a vibrant hub of activity, blending historic architecture with modern amenities. Start your journey at the heart of the city, at the Idaho State Capitol. Located at 700 W Jefferson St, this stunning building is not only the seat of Idaho's government but also a prime example of classical architecture. Guided tours are available, offering insights into Idaho's history and political landscape.

After exploring the Capitol, head to the nearby Old Boise Historic District. This area, centered around 6th and Main Streets, boasts a charming mix of shops, restaurants, and galleries housed in buildings dating back to the late 19th and early 20th centuries. Don't miss Freak Alley Gallery, an outdoor urban art gallery adorned with vibrant murals that change annually, showcasing Boise's artistic spirit.

For those interested in local history and culture, the Boise Art Museum (670 Julia Davis Dr) is a must-visit. With a diverse collection of contemporary art, rotating exhibitions, and educational programs, the museum offers insights into both local and global artistic trends. Check their website for current exhibits and special events.

Basque Block: A Cultural Journey

Boise is home to one of the largest Basque communities in the United States, and the Basque Block, located in downtown Boise on Grove Street between Capitol Boulevard and 6th Street, is the epicenter of this cultural heritage. Start your exploration at the Basque Museum & Cultural Center (611 W Grove St), where exhibits detail the history, traditions, and contributions of the Basque people to Idaho's cultural tapestry.

After visiting the museum, immerse yourself in Basque cuisine at one of the local restaurants. Bar Gernika (202 S Capitol Blvd) offers authentic pintxos (Basque small plates) and hearty entrees in a cozy, pub-like atmosphere. For a taste of tradition, try the chorizo sandwich or the famous lamb grinder.

No visit to the Basque Block is complete without experiencing a traditional Basque festival or event. From the lively Jaialdi festival held every five years to weekly paella dinners and dance performances, the Basque Block offers a year-round celebration of Basque culture that's not to be missed.

Boise River Greenbelt: Nature's Escape in the Heart of the City

For outdoor enthusiasts, the Boise River Greenbelt is a 25-mile scenic pathway that winds along the Boise River, offering stunning views and recreational opportunities. Accessible from multiple points throughout the city, the Greenbelt is perfect for walking, jogging, cycling, or simply relaxing amidst nature.

Start your Greenbelt adventure at Kathryn Albertson Park (1001 N Americana Blvd), a tranquil oasis featuring ponds, waterfalls, and a variety of native flora and fauna. From there, follow the Greenbelt east towards Barber Park (4049 S Eckert Rd), where you can rent a kayak or paddleboard to explore the river at your own pace.

For a family-friendly outing, visit Julia Davis Park (700 S Capitol Blvd), located near downtown Boise. This expansive park not only offers playgrounds, picnic areas, and walking paths but also houses several cultural institutions, including the Boise Art Museum and the Idaho Historical Museum. It's the perfect spot to unwind after a day of exploring downtown Boise.

Boise Foothills: Hiking Trails and Panoramic Views

No visit to Boise is complete without exploring the Boise Foothills, a natural playground for outdoor enthusiasts of all skill levels. With over 190 miles of interconnected trails, the Foothills offer breathtaking views of the city skyline, the Boise River Valley, and the surrounding mountains.

One of the most popular trailheads is located at Camel's Back Park (1200 W Heron St), where you can embark on the Hulls Gulch Interpretive Trail. This moderate hike winds through sagebrush-covered hillsides and offers panoramic vistas of downtown Boise and the Boise River below.

For a more challenging adventure, head to Table Rock Trailhead (6000 E Old Penitentiary Rd), where a steep but rewarding hike leads to the iconic Table Rock Cross. From the summit, enjoy sweeping views of Boise and the Treasure Valley, particularly stunning during sunrise or sunset.

Chapter 1: Exploring Boise's Urban Charms

Downtown Boise: Historic Landmarks and Modern Delights

1. Capitol Boulevard and the Idaho State Capitol

Address: 700 W Jefferson St, Boise, ID 83702

Description: Dominating the skyline with its neoclassical grandeur, the Idaho State Capitol is not just a seat of government but a symbol of Idaho's enduring heritage. Completed in 1920, this majestic building features marble floors, intricate stained glass, and a soaring rotunda adorned with historical murals. Visitors can join guided tours to explore its legislative chambers and learn about Idaho's political history. Don't miss the opportunity to stroll along Capitol Boulevard, lined with trees and offering panoramic views of the Capitol against the backdrop of the Boise foothills.

2. Basque Block

Address: Grove St and Capitol Blvd, Boise, ID 83702

Description: Immerse yourself in Boise's Basque heritage at the lively Basque Block, a cultural enclave steeped in tradition and community spirit. Home to the Basque Museum & Cultural Center, this vibrant neighborhood celebrates the contributions of Basque immigrants through festivals, music, and cuisine. Wander through the Basque Market to sample traditional pintxos and chorizo, or visit the nearby Cyrus Jacobs-Uberuaga Boarding House, a preserved landmark that offers insights into early Basque settlers' lives.

3. Old Boise Historic District

Address: Main St, Boise, ID 83702

Description: Step back in time as you explore the Old Boise Historic District, where charming brick buildings and Victorian-era architecture evoke the city's pioneer past. Start your journey at the historic Pioneer Building, dating back to 1900, which now houses shops and cafes. Wander along 6th and Main Streets to discover boutiques, art galleries, and the iconic Egyptian Theatre, a 1927 movie palace that hosts film screenings, concerts, and community events.

4. Freak Alley Gallery

Address: 210 N 9th St, Boise, ID 83702

Description: A testament to Boise's vibrant arts scene, Freak Alley Gallery is a celebrated outdoor mural space that transforms alleyways into an open-air art gallery. Local and international artists have adorned the walls with colorful and thought-provoking murals, creating a dynamic urban canvas that evolves with each new addition. Take a leisurely stroll through this artistic labyrinth to appreciate its creativity and the diverse perspectives it showcases.

5. Boise River Greenbelt

Address: Multiple access points throughout Downtown Boise

Description: Escape the urban hustle and bustle by exploring the serene Boise River Greenbelt, a 25-mile-long pathway that meanders through Downtown Boise. Perfect for walking, jogging, or cycling, this scenic trail offers tranquil views of the river, shaded pathways, and opportunities for wildlife spotting. Pack a picnic and unwind at one of the greenbelt parks, such as Julia Davis Park or Anne Morrison Park, which also host outdoor concerts and community events during the summer months.

6. Idaho Anne Frank Human Rights Memorial

Address: 777 S 8th St, Boise, ID 83702

Description: Pay homage to human rights at the Idaho Anne Frank Human Rights Memorial, a tranquil sanctuary dedicated to promoting tolerance and justice. Inspired by Anne Frank's message of hope, this contemplative space features quotes from human rights leaders, a life-sized bronze statue of Anne Frank, and a reflecting pool that symbolizes the ongoing struggle for human rights worldwide. The memorial serves as a poignant reminder of Boise's commitment to fostering inclusivity and compassion within its community.

7. Dining and Nightlife

Description: Downtown Boise is a culinary hotspot, offering a diverse array of dining options that cater to every palate. Start your day with a hearty breakfast at Goldy's Breakfast Bistro or The Egg Factory, beloved for their comfort food and locally sourced ingredients. For lunch, head to Fork, where farm-to-table dishes highlight Idaho's agricultural bounty, or grab a quick bite at the Boise Fry Company for customizable potato-centric meals.

Nightlife: As the sun sets, Downtown Boise comes alive with vibrant nightlife options. Sip on craft cocktails at The

Modern Hotel and Bar or Bardenay Restaurant & Distillery, Idaho's first distillery since Prohibition. Music enthusiasts can catch live performances at the Neurolux Lounge or the Reef Boise, where local bands and touring artists entertain crowds with a variety of genres.

Boise River Greenbelt: A Serene Escape in the Heart of the City

Overview and History

The Boise River Greenbelt traces its origins back to the early 1960s when city planners envisioned a green corridor that would enhance recreational opportunities and protect the river's ecosystem. Over the decades, careful development and community support have transformed the Greenbelt into a beloved feature of Boise's landscape, attracting locals and visitors alike year-round.

Exploring the Greenbelt

The Greenbelt is more than just a trail; it's a tapestry of experiences waiting to be explored. Whether you're seeking a leisurely stroll, a bike ride, or a quiet spot for picnicking, each segment of the Greenbelt offers unique sights and activities.

Main Sections and Highlights

1. Downtown Boise to Barber Park

Begin your journey at the heart of downtown Boise, where the Greenbelt starts near the 9th Street Bridge. Follow the river southwards past Julia Davis Park, where you can explore the Boise Art Museum or simply relax amidst the lush gardens. Continuing eastward, the path leads to Anne Morrison Park, a popular spot for families with playgrounds and sports fields. As you approach Barber Park, nature enthusiasts can embark on rafting adventures down the Boise River, navigating gentle rapids while enjoying scenic views of the foothills.

2. Barber Park to Warm Springs

From Barber Park, the Greenbelt meanders northeast towards Warm Springs Avenue, offering a tranquil stretch lined with cottonwood trees and riverside vistas. This section is ideal for birdwatching, with opportunities to spot herons, osprey, and other wildlife that call the riverbanks home. History buffs will appreciate the historic Warm Springs Avenue, renowned for its early 20th-century mansions and the geothermal springs that gave the area its name.

3. Warm Springs to Lucky Peak Dam

Continuing eastward, the Greenbelt passes through Marianne Williams Park, a peaceful retreat with picnic areas and access to the river for fishing enthusiasts. As you approach Lucky Peak State Park and Dam, the landscape transitions to rugged terrain dotted with sagebrush and juniper, offering hikers and mountain bikers a chance to explore trails that wind through the Boise Foothills.

Points of Interest and Activities

Throughout the Boise River Greenbelt, several points of interest invite exploration:

Idaho Anne Frank Human Rights Memorial: Located near the 9th Street Bridge, this memorial offers a contemplative space dedicated to promoting human rights and social justice.

Boise Zoo: Situated adjacent to Julia Davis Park, the zoo features over 300 animals from around the world and offers educational programs for visitors of all ages.

Eagle Island State Park: Although slightly off the main Greenbelt path, this park is a short drive away and provides opportunities for swimming, picnicking, and wildlife viewing along the Boise River.

Practical Tips and Visitor Information

Access Points: The Greenbelt can be accessed from multiple points throughout Boise, with parking available at various parks and trailheads.

Trail Etiquette: Cyclists and pedestrians share the path, so be mindful of others and follow posted guidelines.

Seasonal Considerations: While the Greenbelt is open year-round, spring and fall offer pleasant weather for outdoor activities, while summer brings opportunities for water sports and river activities.

Safety: Stay on designated paths and be aware of your surroundings, especially near the riverbanks where conditions can change rapidly during spring runoff or heavy rain.

Basque Block: A Cultural Journey through Boise's Basque Heritage

History and Heritage

Boise's Basque community traces its roots back to the late 1800s when Basque immigrants began arriving in Idaho seeking opportunities in sheep herding and agriculture. Drawn by the promise of fertile land and economic stability, these pioneers brought with them a distinct culture and language that would leave an indelible mark on the state's identity.

The Basque Block, centered around Grove Street between Capitol Boulevard and 6th Street, is home to several key institutions that preserve and celebrate this heritage. The Basque Museum & Cultural Center serves as the focal point, offering exhibits that chronicle the journey of Basque immigrants to Idaho and their contributions to the state's development.

Exploring the Basque Block

Begin your journey through the Basque Block at the Basque Museum & Cultural Center (611 W Grove St). Here, artifacts, photographs, and interactive displays offer insights into the Basque experience in Idaho. Learn about traditional Basque festivals like Jaialdi, which draws Basque communities from around the world to Boise every five years in celebration of their culture.

Adjacent to the museum is the Cyrus Jacobs-Uberuaga Boarding House (607 W Grove St), a historic landmark that once provided lodging for Basque immigrants arriving in Boise. Today, it stands as a testament to the hardships and triumphs of those early settlers, preserved with period furnishings and exhibits that recreate life in the late 19th and early 20th centuries.

Cuisine and Dining

No visit to the Basque Block is complete without savoring the flavors of Basque cuisine. Head to Leku Ona (117 S 6th St), a beloved restaurant serving traditional Basque dishes such as paella, chorizo, and pintxos—small, flavorful appetizers that pair perfectly with a glass of Basque wine or cider. The ambiance here transports you to the Basque Country with its warm hospitality and authentic recipes passed down through generations.

For a taste of Basque sweets and treats, stop by The Basque Market (608 W Grove St). This bustling market offers a selection of imported Basque cheeses, meats, and pastries, alongside local favorites like chorizo sandwiches and Basque-style chocolates. Grab a seat at their outdoor patio during warmer months and enjoy live music and community gatherings that reflect the Basque spirit of camaraderie and conviviality.

Cultural Events and Festivals

Throughout the year, the Basque Block comes alive with cultural events that celebrate Basque traditions and customs. Don't miss the San Inazio Festival held annually in late July, featuring Basque music, dance performances, and a lively pelota tournament—a traditional Basque sport similar to handball. The festival attracts Basque communities from across the United States and Europe, offering visitors a unique opportunity to immerse themselves in Basque culture right in the heart of Boise.

Exploring Beyond the Basque Block

Extend your exploration of Boise's Basque heritage by visiting nearby attractions that pay homage to this resilient community. Just a short drive from downtown, you'll find the Boise Basque Center (601 Grove St), a hub for Basque cultural activities and community gatherings. Check their calendar for language classes, folk dancing lessons, and special events that foster a deeper understanding of Basque traditions among locals and visitors alike.

Chapter 2: Outdoor Escapes

Boise Foothills: Hiking Trails and Panoramic Views

Exploring the Trails

The Boise Foothills boast a network of trails that wind through sagebrush-covered hillsides, rolling hills, and rocky outcrops. Whether you're looking for a leisurely stroll or a challenging hike, there's a trail to suit every preference.

Hulls Gulch Reserve

One of the most popular entry points into the Boise Foothills is Hulls Gulch Reserve, located just minutes from downtown. This expansive reserve offers a variety of trails that wind through scenic landscapes and provide stunning views of the city skyline below.

Trailhead Address: Hulls Gulch Reserve Trailhead, 3001 N 36th St, Boise, ID 83703

Trail Options: The Hulls Gulch Interpretive Trail is a great starting point, offering a gentle ascent through wildflowers and occasional wildlife sightings. For a longer hike, connect to the Crestline Trail, which leads to sweeping panoramas of the Treasure Valley and beyond.

Camels Back Park

Another favorite among locals and visitors alike is Camels Back Park, renowned for its iconic Camel's Back Ridge trail. This moderately challenging hike rewards adventurers with stunning views of downtown Boise and the surrounding mountains.

Trailhead Address: Camels Back Park Trailhead, 1200 Heron St, Boise, ID 83702

Trail Highlights: The Camel's Back Ridge Trail ascends steadily through rocky terrain, culminating in a ridge that offers unparalleled 360-degree views of the city and the Boise River winding through the valley below. Sunset hikes are particularly spectacular, as the fading light paints the landscape in hues of orange and pink.

Table Rock

For a more strenuous trek and a glimpse into Boise's history, head to Table Rock. This prominent landmark overlooks the city and is crowned by the iconic Table Rock Cross, a symbol of Boise's heritage.

Trailhead Address: Table Rock Trailhead, Old Penitentiary Rd, Boise, ID 83712

Trail Details: The Table Rock Trail begins at the Old Penitentiary and ascends steeply through rugged terrain. Along the way, interpretive signs provide insights into the area's geological and cultural significance. At the summit, hikers are rewarded with expansive views of downtown Boise, the Boise River, and the distant Owyhee Mountains.

Wildlife and Natural Diversity

Beyond the panoramic views, the Boise Foothills are home to a rich diversity of flora and fauna. Keep an eye out for mule deer, jackrabbits, and a variety of bird species, including golden eagles and red-tailed hawks. Springtime brings vibrant wildflowers, carpeting the hillsides in hues of purple, yellow, and white.

Tips for Visitors

Seasonal Considerations: While accessible year-round, the best times to explore the Boise Foothills are spring and fall when temperatures are mild and wildflowers or autumn foliage enhance the scenery.

Safety Precautions: Wear sturdy footwear, carry plenty of water, and be mindful of local wildlife. Trail conditions can vary, especially after rain or snowmelt.

Leave No Trace: Respect the natural environment by packing out trash, staying on designated trails, and minimizing your impact on wildlife habitats.

Connecting with Boise's Natural Beauty

The Boise Foothills offer more than just hiking opportunities; they provide a gateway to understanding Boise's unique geography and natural beauty. Whether you're an avid hiker, a nature enthusiast, or simply seeking moments of solitude amidst stunning landscapes, the foothills deliver an experience that is both invigorating and enlightening.

Bogus Basin: Year-Round Mountain Adventure

Winter Wonderland: Skiing and Snowboarding

Winter transforms Bogus Basin into a snowy wonderland, drawing outdoor enthusiasts from near and far. With an elevation ranging from 5,800 to 7,582 feet, Bogus Basin boasts a reliable snowpack that ensures optimal skiing and snowboarding conditions from late November through April.

Skiing and Snowboarding: Bogus Basin features 91 named trails spread across 2,600 acres of skiable terrain, catering to all skill levels. From gentle slopes ideal for beginners to challenging runs that thrill advanced skiers, every descent promises breathtaking views of the Boise National Forest.

Terrain Parks: For those craving aerial stunts and rail slides, Bogus Basin's terrain parks deliver. The Shafer Butte Terrain Park is a popular spot for freestyle enthusiasts, offering a variety of features designed to challenge and inspire.

Lifts and Accessibility: Seven lifts—including a high-speed quad and multiple surface lifts—ensure quick and convenient access to the slopes. Lift tickets and season passes can be purchased online or at the resort, with options for night skiing under the stars on select evenings.

Lessons and Programs: Whether you're learning the basics or honing advanced techniques, Bogus Basin's ski school offers lessons for all ages and abilities. Private and group lessons, as well as specialized programs like adaptive skiing, cater to diverse learning styles and needs.

Summer Escapes: Hiking, Biking, and More

When the snow melts, Bogus Basin transitions into a playground for outdoor adventurers seeking alpine beauty and fresh mountain air.

Hiking Trails: Explore a network of trails that wind through forests of fir and pine, offering scenic overlooks and opportunities to spot local wildlife. Popular hikes include the Shafer Butte Trail, which leads to the summit with sweeping views of the Treasure Valley below.

Mountain Biking: Bogus Basin's trails transform into thrilling mountain biking routes, ranging from gentle paths suitable for beginners to technical descents that challenge even seasoned riders. Bike rentals and guided tours are available at the resort, ensuring everyone can enjoy the ride.

Scenic Chairlift Rides: Experience the beauty of Bogus Basin from a different perspective with scenic chairlift rides. Ascend to higher elevations and soak in panoramic views of the Boise foothills and beyond, perfect for photography enthusiasts and nature lovers alike.

Summer Events and Activities: From music festivals and yoga retreats to nature walks and disc golf tournaments, Bogus Basin's summer calendar brims with events that celebrate the outdoors and community spirit. Check the resort's website for updated schedules and details.

Dining and Amenities

Pioneer Lodge: Located at the base area, the Pioneer Lodge offers dining options ranging from hearty meals to quick bites, perfect for fueling up before hitting the slopes or winding down after a day of adventure.

Simo's Summer Shack: A favorite spot during the warmer months, Simo's Summer Shack serves up delicious fare and refreshing beverages on its outdoor patio, complete with live music and a relaxed atmosphere.

Rental Services: Whether you need ski gear in winter or mountain bikes in summer, Bogus Basin's rental shop provides quality equipment for all ages and sizes. Advanced reservations are recommended during peak seasons to ensure availability.

Getting There

Address: Bogus Basin Road, Boise, ID 83702

Directions: From downtown Boise, take Highway 55 north for approximately 16 miles. Follow signs for Bogus Basin and continue on Bogus Basin Road until you reach the resort's main parking area.

Parking: Ample parking is available at the resort, with designated areas for day visitors and overnight guests. Be sure to check parking fees and regulations, especially during peak seasons.

Tips for Visitors

Weather Preparedness: Idaho's mountain weather can change rapidly. Pack layers, sunscreen, and sunglasses year-round.

Reservations: During winter, consider purchasing lift tickets and rentals online in advance to skip lines and ensure availability.

Trail Etiquette: Respect trail signs and closures. Be aware of wildlife and adhere to Leave No Trace principles to preserve Bogus Basin's natural beauty.

Julia Davis Park: Green Oasis with Museums and Attractions

Exploring the Park's Natural Beauty

Julia Davis Park's allure begins with its picturesque setting along the Boise River Greenbelt, a 25-mile pathway that winds through the city, offering cyclists, joggers, and walkers a scenic route to explore. The park itself is a lush expanse of greenery, with sprawling lawns, mature trees providing ample shade, and winding pathways that beckon visitors to stroll and unwind amidst nature's embrace. Benches scattered throughout the park offer perfect spots for quiet contemplation or simply enjoying the view of the river flowing gently by.

Cultural and Historical Landmarks

One of the defining features of Julia Davis Park is its collection of museums and historical sites, each adding layers of depth to the visitor experience:

Boise Art Museum (670 Julia Davis Dr, Boise, ID 83702):

Nestled within the park, the Boise Art Museum (BAM) showcases a diverse collection of contemporary art and rotating exhibitions that highlight both regional and international artists. Established in 1937, BAM has grown to become a cultural hub, offering visitors a chance to engage with art through educational programs, workshops, and special events. The museum's architecture itself is noteworthy, blending modern design with Boise's natural surroundings.

Idaho State Historical Museum (610 Julia Davis Dr, Boise, ID 83702):

Just steps away from the Boise Art Museum, the Idaho State Historical Museum offers a compelling journey through Idaho's past. Housed in a striking building that echoes the region's architectural heritage, the museum's exhibits cover topics ranging from Native American history to pioneer life and modern-day Idaho. Interactive displays and immersive exhibits make this museum a must-visit for history enthusiasts of all ages.

Idaho Black History Museum (508 Julia Davis Dr, Boise, ID 83702):

Located near the entrance of Julia Davis Park, the Idaho Black History Museum honors the contributions and experiences of African Americans in Idaho. Housed in the historic St. Paul Baptist Church building, the museum features exhibits that explore the struggles and triumphs of Idaho's Black community, highlighting their impact on the state's cultural and social fabric.

Recreational Activities and Amenities

Julia Davis Park offers a myriad of recreational opportunities that cater to visitors of all ages and interests:

Zoo Boise (355 Julia Davis Dr, Boise, ID 83702): Situated within the park, Zoo Boise is a family-friendly attraction that houses a diverse collection of animals from around the world. The zoo is committed to conservation and education, offering interactive exhibits, keeper talks, and special events throughout the year. Visitors can get up close with species ranging from African lions to North American river otters in habitats designed to mimic their natural environments.

Kathryn Albertson Park: Adjacent to Julia Davis Park, Kathryn Albertson Park offers additional green space and tranquil walking paths around a series of ponds. This park is known for its resident waterfowl, including ducks and geese, making it a peaceful spot for birdwatching and picnicking.

Events and Community Gatherings

Throughout the year, Julia Davis Park plays host to a variety of community events and festivals that showcase Boise's vibrant cultural scene:

Art in the Park: Held annually in September, Art in the Park is one of Boise's premier cultural events, featuring over 200 artists showcasing their work amidst the scenic backdrop of Julia Davis Park. Visitors can browse and purchase original artworks ranging from paintings to sculptures, while enjoying live music, food vendors, and family-friendly activities.

Shakespeare Festival: Each summer, the Idaho Shakespeare Festival brings the works of William Shakespeare to life in an outdoor amphitheater within the park. The festival attracts theater enthusiasts from across the region, offering performances of classic plays under the stars against the picturesque Boise skyline.

Practical Information for Visitors

Julia Davis Park is open year-round and admission to most areas of the park is free, though some attractions like Zoo Boise may have entrance fees. Parking is available throughout the park and along nearby streets, with accessible parking spaces for visitors with disabilities. The park's central location within Boise makes it easily accessible by car, bicycle via the Greenbelt, or on foot from downtown Boise.

Chapter 3: Cultural Delights

Idaho State Capitol: Iconic Architecture and History

History and Construction

The story of the Idaho State Capitol begins in the late 19th century when Boise was selected as the capital of the newly established Idaho Territory in 1864. Initially, governmental operations were housed in various makeshift locations until plans for a permanent capitol building took shape.

In 1905, after years of deliberation and planning, construction on the current capitol building commenced. Designed by renowned architect John E. Tourtellotte in the neoclassical style, the Idaho State Capitol was envisioned to reflect the aspirations and values of the growing state. The project was ambitious, incorporating locally sourced materials and skilled labor to ensure both quality and longevity.

The construction of the Capitol faced numerous challenges, including funding issues and the complexities of architectural design. However, these obstacles were overcome through the dedication of Idaho's citizens and the vision of its leaders, culminating in the completion of the building in 1920. Since then, the Capitol has undergone several renovations and expansions to accommodate the evolving needs of Idaho's government and preserve its historic integrity.

Architectural Splendor

Visitors to the Idaho State Capitol are greeted by its imposing facade, characterized by classical columns, a central dome, and intricate detailing that reflects the craftsmanship of its era. The exterior is primarily clad in sandstone quarried from nearby Table Rock, giving the building a warm, earthy hue that harmonizes with Boise's natural surroundings.

Entering the Capitol through its grand entrance, visitors are welcomed into a rotunda adorned with symbolic artwork and historical exhibits that trace Idaho's journey from territorial status to statehood. The interior spaces are designed to inspire awe, with soaring ceilings, marble floors, and ornate furnishings that evoke a sense of dignity and purpose.

One of the Capitol's most striking features is its central dome, rising to a height of 208 feet and crowned by a statue known as "Winged Victory." This iconic figure, crafted from copper and covered in gold leaf, symbolizes Idaho's triumphs and aspirations. The dome's interior is adorned with murals depicting scenes from Idaho's history, painted by artist Edgar S. Paxson, further enriching the Capitol's cultural significance.

Exploring the Capitol

A visit to the Idaho State Capitol offers a multifaceted experience that combines architectural splendor with historical insight and civic engagement. Guided tours, led by knowledgeable docents, provide visitors with a deeper understanding of the Capitol's design, construction, and role in Idaho's governance.

The Capitol's public spaces include legislative chambers where Idaho's lawmakers convene to debate and enact laws that shape the state's future. Visitors can observe legislative sessions in progress, gaining firsthand insight into the democratic process and the issues facing Idaho's communities.

For those interested in Idaho's political history, the Capitol houses a wealth of archival materials, including documents, photographs, and artifacts that chronicle the state's development over the decades. Exhibits highlight key milestones such as Idaho's role in women's suffrage and its contributions to agriculture, mining, and environmental conservation.

Events and Public Programs

Throughout the year, the Idaho State Capitol hosts a variety of events and public programs that engage visitors of all ages. Educational workshops, lectures by historians, and special exhibitions offer opportunities to delve deeper into Idaho's cultural heritage and civic responsibilities.

One of the Capitol's most cherished traditions is its annual Statehood Day celebration, held on July 3rd to commemorate Idaho's admission to the Union in 1890. The event features live music, historical reenactments, and family-friendly activities that celebrate Idaho's diverse communities and shared history.

Additionally, the Capitol's grounds serve as a gathering place for civic demonstrations, public rallies, and cultural festivals that reflect the vibrancy and diversity of Idaho's population. These events underscore the Capitol's role not only as a seat of government but also as a hub of community engagement and democratic discourse.

Visiting Information

Address: 700 W Jefferson St, Boise, ID 83702

Hours: Monday-Friday, 8:00 AM - 5:00 PM (Closed on state holidays)

Admission: Free

Guided Tours: Available Monday-Friday at scheduled times; reservations recommended for groups

Accessibility: The Capitol is wheelchair accessible, with ramps and elevators provided for ease of navigation

Boise Art Museum: Contemporary Art and Exhibitions

History and Mission

Founded by a group of local artists and enthusiasts, BAM was initially established to provide a platform for regional artists to showcase their works. Over time, it has grown to encompass a broader scope, featuring national and international artists while maintaining its commitment to supporting the local art community. The museum's mission is to enrich the lives of Boise residents and visitors through engaging exhibitions, educational opportunities, and outreach programs that promote visual arts appreciation and creativity.

Exhibition Spaces

BAM's exhibition spaces are designed to immerse visitors in a world of artistic innovation and exploration. The museum boasts several galleries that showcase a rotating selection of contemporary artworks, ranging from paintings and sculptures to multimedia installations and interactive exhibits. Each gallery is curated with meticulous attention to detail, creating thematic narratives that invite viewers to ponder and engage with the art on display.

Highlights of Permanent Collection

While BAM is renowned for its temporary exhibitions, it also houses a notable permanent collection that spans various genres and mediums. The collection includes works by both established masters and emerging artists, reflecting the museum's commitment to preserving and celebrating artistic heritage while embracing contemporary trends. Notable pieces include sculptures by local artist James Castle and paintings by renowned American modernists.

Current and Upcoming Exhibitions

Visitors to BAM can always expect something new and exciting, as the museum regularly updates its exhibition schedule to showcase the latest trends in contemporary art. Recent exhibitions have explored themes such as environmental sustainability, social justice, and technological innovation, providing a platform for artists to address pressing issues through their work. Upcoming exhibitions include a retrospective of multimedia artist Rebecca Horn and a showcase of emerging Idaho artists selected through a juried competition.

Educational Programs and Outreach

BAM is committed to fostering a deeper understanding and appreciation of art through its robust educational programs and outreach initiatives. The museum offers guided tours, artist talks, and hands-on workshops designed to engage audiences of all ages and backgrounds. School groups and community organizations are invited to participate in specially curated programs that highlight the intersection of art, culture, and education.

Visitor Experience

A visit to BAM is more than just a passive viewing experience; it's an opportunity to immerse oneself in creativity and inspiration. The museum's inviting atmosphere, coupled with its knowledgeable staff and volunteer docents, ensures that every visitor feels welcomed and informed. Interactive exhibits and multimedia installations encourage exploration and dialogue, making BAM a cultural hub where ideas and perspectives converge.

Planning Your Visit

For those planning a visit to BAM, here are a few practical tips to enhance your experience:

Hours and Admission: BAM is open Tuesday through Sunday, with extended hours on Thursdays. Admission prices vary, with discounts available for seniors, students, and members of the military. Children under 12 enjoy free admission.

Accessibility: The museum is wheelchair accessible, with designated parking and ramps for easy entry. Accessible restrooms and elevators are available throughout the facility.

Parking: On-site parking is available for museum visitors, with additional parking options nearby in Julia Davis Park.

Dining and Amenities: While BAM does not have a dedicated restaurant, several dining options can be found nearby in downtown Boise and the North End district. The museum offers a gift shop where visitors can purchase art-inspired souvenirs and books.

Idaho Botanical Garden: Blooms and Beauty in Every Season

History and Overview

Founded in 1984, the Idaho Botanical Garden began as a grassroots effort by local garden enthusiasts and community leaders who envisioned a place where residents and visitors could connect with nature and learn about sustainable gardening practices. Over the decades, the garden has grown from a modest plot to a premier botanical attraction, thanks to dedicated volunteers, generous donors, and collaborative partnerships with horticultural experts.

The garden's mission extends beyond mere aesthetics; it serves as a vital educational resource, offering workshops, tours, and community programs that promote environmental stewardship and conservation. Today, the Idaho Botanical Garden welcomes thousands of visitors annually, each drawn to its tranquil pathways, diverse plant collections, and engaging events.

Exploring the Garden

Upon entering the Idaho Botanical Garden, visitors are greeted by a harmonious blend of formal gardens, themed displays, and natural landscapes that reflect Idaho's diverse ecosystems. The garden is thoughtfully divided into distinct areas, each highlighting unique plant species and gardening techniques suited to the region's climate.

Formal Gardens and Landscapes

One of the garden's most beloved features is its collection of formal gardens, meticulously designed to showcase both native and exotic plants. The English Garden, with its manicured lawns and perennial borders, evokes a sense of timeless elegance reminiscent of classic European estates. Visitors can stroll along gravel paths lined with roses, lavender, and delphiniums, pausing to admire sculptures and ornamental fountains that punctuate the landscape.

Nearby, the Meditation Garden offers a tranquil retreat characterized by Zen-inspired elements, including cascading water features and carefully placed rocks. Here, visitors can unwind amidst a tapestry of ferns, Japanese maples, and flowering shrubs chosen for their calming effect and seasonal interest.

For those seeking inspiration for their own gardens, the Herb Garden provides a sensory experience that celebrates culinary and medicinal plants. Fragrant herbs like basil, thyme, and lavender thrive in raised beds, while educational signage offers insights into their historical uses and cultivation tips for home gardeners.

Seasonal Highlights

One of the Idaho Botanical Garden's greatest charms lies in its ever-changing tapestry of blooms and foliage, which transform with the seasons. Spring heralds the arrival of cherry blossoms in the Asian Garden, where delicate petals carpet the ground beneath ancient trees imported from Japan. Tulips and daffodils burst into color across the grounds, creating a vibrant backdrop for seasonal events like the Spring Plant Sale and Garden Festival.

Summer brings a riot of colors to the Rose Garden, where hundreds of varieties bloom in a symphony of scents and hues. Visitors can attend twilight concerts amidst the fragrant blooms or join guided tours that reveal the garden's historical significance and the art of rose cultivation.

Autumn casts a golden glow over the Idaho Botanical Garden, as deciduous trees transform into fiery hues of red, orange, and yellow. The Native Plant Garden showcases indigenous species like sagebrush and bitterbrush, their muted tones contrasting with the vivid palette of ornamental grasses and late-blooming perennials.

Winter invites a different kind of beauty, as the garden shimmers under a blanket of snow and ice. Evergreen conifers provide year-round structure, their branches laden with snowflakes that catch the winter sun. The Holiday Lights display transforms the garden into a magical wonderland, with thousands of twinkling lights illuminating paths and reflecting off icy ponds.

Special Collections and Exhibits

Beyond its seasonal displays, the Idaho Botanical Garden is home to several specialized collections that showcase the diversity of plant life from around the world. The Lewis and Clark Native Plant Garden pays homage to the expedition's botanical discoveries, featuring species encountered during their historic journey across the American West.

The Children's Adventure Garden offers interactive exhibits and hands-on activities designed to foster a love of nature in young visitors. Here, children can explore themed play areas, discover hidden sculptures, and learn about pollinators through immersive educational displays.

For enthusiasts of succulents and desert plants, the Cactus and Succulent Garden showcases a stunning array of drought-tolerant species from arid regions. Barrel cacti, agaves, and prickly pears thrive in rocky, well-drained soil, their architectural forms creating a striking contrast against the backdrop of Idaho's lush greenery.

Educational Programs and Events

The Idaho Botanical Garden is committed to promoting environmental literacy and sustainability through a variety of educational programs and events. Workshops on organic gardening, water-wise landscaping, and composting are offered throughout the year, providing participants with practical skills and eco-friendly solutions for home and community gardens.

Guided tours led by knowledgeable docents offer deeper insights into the garden's history, plant collections, and seasonal highlights. Visitors can explore themed tours focused on horticultural techniques, wildlife habitats, or the cultural significance of plants in Idaho's history.

Special events enrich the garden's calendar, inviting visitors to celebrate seasonal milestones and cultural traditions. The Harvest Festival celebrates Idaho's agricultural heritage with pumpkin patches, hayrides, and farm-to-table tastings, while the Summer Concert Series showcases local musicians against a backdrop of blooming gardens and starlit skies.

Visitor Information

The Idaho Botanical Garden is located at 2355 N Old Penitentiary Rd, Boise, ID 83712, just minutes from downtown Boise. It is open year-round, with seasonal hours that vary according to daylight and special events. Admission fees support the garden's maintenance and educational programs, with discounts available for seniors, students, and members of the Idaho Botanical Garden Society.

The garden is wheelchair-accessible, with paved pathways that meander through most areas of the grounds. Visitors are encouraged to wear comfortable footwear and dress according to the season, as weather conditions can vary throughout the day.

Ample parking is available on-site, with designated areas for bicycles and electric vehicles. Picnicking is permitted in designated areas, allowing visitors to enjoy a leisurely meal amidst the garden's natural beauty. Restrooms and drinking fountains are conveniently located throughout the grounds for visitor comfort and convenience.

Chapter 4: Dining and Local Flavors

Boise's Best Eateries: From Farm-to-Table to Global Cuisine

1. Fork

Located in the heart of downtown Boise at 199 N 8th St, Fork has become a local favorite for its commitment to sourcing ingredients from local farms and producers. The restaurant's rustic-chic ambiance sets the stage for a menu that celebrates Idaho's bounty, featuring dishes like Snake River Farms Wagyu Beef and Idaho Trout. Don't miss their signature Fork Salad, a colorful ensemble of seasonal greens and vegetables drizzled with house-made dressings.

2. State & Lemp

Nestled in the historic North End neighborhood at 2870 W State St, State & Lemp offers a unique dining experience that blends artistry with culinary innovation. Known for its ever-changing prix fixe menu, State & Lemp focuses on seasonal ingredients and creative presentations that showcase the chef's meticulous attention to detail. Each course is a journey of flavors, carefully curated to surprise and delight diners.

3. Barbacoa Grill

For a taste of Latin American flavors with a touch of elegance, visit Barbacoa Grill at 276 Bobwhite Ct. This upscale restaurant boasts a menu inspired by the cuisines of Mexico, South America, and the Caribbean. Indulge in dishes like their famous Chilean Sea Bass with tropical salsa or their savory Oaxacan Mole Chicken. The restaurant's vibrant atmosphere and extensive tequila selection add to the dining experience.

4. Juniper

Located at 211 N 8th St, Juniper combines the best of Northwest cuisine with a modern twist. The restaurant's commitment to sustainability is evident in its seasonal menu, which features locally sourced ingredients and innovative dishes. Start your meal with their artisanal cheese board featuring Idaho cheeses, followed by their Cedar Plank Salmon or Bison Meatloaf, both showcasing the region's flavors in every bite.

5. Chandlers Steakhouse

Situated in downtown Boise at 981 W Grove St, Chandlers Steakhouse is renowned for its prime steaks, seafood, and live jazz music. Step into an atmosphere of old-world elegance as you savor dishes like their USDA Prime Ribeye or Alaskan King Crab Legs. Pair your meal with selections from their extensive wine list or indulge in a handcrafted cocktail from the bar.

6. The Basque Market

Experience the flavors of the Basque Country at The Basque Market, located at 608 W Grove St. This cozy market and deli offers a taste of Spain with its selection of pintxos (Basque-style tapas) and hearty paellas. Grab a seat at the outdoor patio or join the lively atmosphere inside as you enjoy specialties like their Chorizo Sandwich or Bacalao Pil Pil.

7. Boise Fry Company

For a taste of Idaho's most beloved crop, visit Boise Fry Company at 204 N Capitol Blvd. This casual eatery celebrates the humble potato with a menu that allows diners to customize their fries with a variety of seasonings and dipping sauces. Pair your fries with a gourmet burger made from locally sourced beef, turkey, or even a vegetarian patty for a satisfying meal.

8. Bittercreek Alehouse

Located at 246 N 8th St, Bittercreek Alehouse is a haven for beer enthusiasts and foodies alike. This gastropub emphasizes sustainable practices with a menu that highlights organic, locally sourced ingredients. Enjoy their Beer-Battered Fish and Chips or their Bison Burger paired with one of their many craft beers on tap. The pub's laid-back atmosphere and commitment to eco-friendly dining make it a favorite among locals.

9. Lemon Tree Co.

If you're looking for a healthy and delicious meal, head to Lemon Tree Co. at 224 N 10th St. This vibrant cafe specializes in fresh salads, sandwiches, and smoothies made from locally sourced ingredients. Try their Avocado Toast with a twist or their Quinoa Bowl topped with seasonal vegetables. Their commitment to sustainability and community-driven dining makes Lemon Tree Co. a popular choice for health-conscious diners.

10. Tasso

Located at 401 S 8th St, Tasso brings a taste of the Mediterranean to downtown Boise with its flavorful dishes and warm hospitality. Inspired by the cuisine of Greece, Turkey, and Lebanon, Tasso offers a menu that highlights traditional flavors with a modern twist. Indulge in their Lamb Gyro or their Mezze Platter featuring hummus, tzatziki, and stuffed grape leaves. Pair your meal with a glass of Greek wine or a refreshing Mediterranean cocktail.

North End District: Quaint Cafes and Neighborhood Charm

Exploring Hyde Park

At the heart of the North End lies Hyde Park, a picturesque gathering place brimming with character and charm. As you stroll along North 13th Street, the ambiance shifts to a quaint village feel, where historic architecture blends seamlessly with modern amenities.

1. Hyde Perk Coffee House

Start your exploration at Hyde Perk Coffee House, located at 1507 North 13th Street. This cozy cafe exudes warmth with its rustic decor and inviting aroma of freshly brewed coffee. Locals gather here for their morning caffeine fix or leisurely afternoon chats over artisanal pastries and locally sourced snacks. The outdoor patio, shaded by towering trees, provides a perfect spot to soak in the neighborhood ambiance.

2. Camel's Back Park

Just a short walk from Hyde Park is Camel's Back Park, a beloved green space offering panoramic views of Boise's skyline and the foothills beyond. This expansive park features picnic areas, playgrounds, and hiking trails that wind through native flora, making it a popular retreat for families and outdoor enthusiasts alike.

Cafes and Eateries

3. Goody's Soda Fountain & Candy Store

For a nostalgic treat, head to Goody's Soda Fountain & Candy Store at 1502 North 13th Street. Step inside this vintage establishment, where classic soda floats, handmade chocolates, and old-fashioned candies evoke a sense of nostalgia. The retro decor and friendly service add to the charm, making it a delightful stop for both young and old.

4. Parilla Grill

Craving something savory? Parilla Grill, located at 1512 North 13th Street, is a local favorite known for its build-your-own burritos and bowls. With fresh ingredients and a laid-back atmosphere, it's the perfect spot for a casual lunch or dinner. Choose from a variety of proteins, vegetables, and house-made salsas to customize your meal just the way you like it.

5. Sun Ray Cafe

Continuing down the street, you'll find Sun Ray Cafe at 1602 North 13th Street, a cozy eatery that blends artistry with culinary passion. This charming cafe features a menu of locally sourced ingredients crafted into creative dishes that reflect Boise's farm-to-table ethos. Whether you're indulging in their signature brunch offerings or enjoying an evening meal paired with local wines, Sun Ray Cafe promises a memorable dining experience.

Local Shops and Boutiques

6. North End Organic Nursery

For green thumbs and garden enthusiasts, North End Organic Nursery at 2350 Hill Road offers a unique shopping experience. This boutique nursery specializes in organic plants, heirloom seeds, and eco-friendly gardening supplies. Wander through their lush garden displays, attend a workshop on sustainable gardening practices, or seek advice from knowledgeable staff passionate about cultivating a greener community.

7. Rediscovered Bookshop

Book lovers won't want to miss Rediscovered Bookshop at 180 North 8th Street, a literary haven nestled in the heart of the North End. Browse shelves stocked with a curated selection of new releases, bestsellers, and local authors' works. The cozy atmosphere invites you to linger, whether you're attending a book signing event, joining a book club discussion, or simply discovering your next great read.

Cultural Attractions

8. Boise Contemporary Theater

Embrace Boise's thriving arts scene at Boise Contemporary Theater, located at 854 Fulton Street. This intimate venue showcases innovative performances ranging from thought-provoking dramas to cutting-edge comedies. With a commitment to producing new works and supporting local talent, Boise Contemporary Theater invites audiences to engage with compelling stories that resonate long after the curtain falls.

9. Idaho Shakespeare Festival

During the summer months, venture to the Idaho Shakespeare Festival at 5657 Warm Springs Avenue for an unforgettable outdoor theater experience. Set against the backdrop of the Boise River and the foothills, this renowned festival presents Shakespearean classics, contemporary plays, and musical productions under the starlit sky. Pack a picnic, settle into your seat, and immerse yourself in the magic of live theater surrounded by Idaho's natural beauty.

Community Events and Festivals

10. Hyde Park Street Fair

Every September, the Hyde Park Street Fair transforms North 13th Street into a lively celebration of art, music, and community spirit. Join locals and visitors as they browse artisan booths, savor international cuisine from food vendors, and enjoy live performances by local bands. With activities for all ages and a festive atmosphere, this neighborhood fair captures the essence of Boise's North End.

11. First Thursday

On the first Thursday of each month, Boise's art scene comes alive during First Thursday gallery walks. Explore North End galleries, studios, and boutiques as they open their doors to showcase local artwork, host artist receptions, and offer special promotions. Stroll along North 13th Street and beyond, discovering hidden gems and meeting artists who shape Boise's cultural landscape.

Boise Brewing: Craft Beer and Local Brews to Savor

History and Vision

Boise Brewing was established in 2014 by founders Collin Rudeen and Lance Chavez, who shared a passion for brewing and a deep love for their hometown. What started as a modest brewery in a renovated warehouse has grown into a cornerstone of Boise's brewing culture, known for its commitment to sustainability and community engagement.

Located at 521 West Broad Street, Boise Brewing's taproom welcomes guests with an inviting atmosphere that blends industrial charm with modern comfort. The brewery's mission goes beyond crafting exceptional beer; it extends to supporting local causes through their "Pints for a Purpose" program, where a portion of proceeds from select beers goes to community nonprofits.

The Brewing Process

Stepping into Boise Brewing, visitors are greeted by the sights, sounds, and aromas of the brewing process. The brewery operates on a 7-barrel brewing system, allowing for a hands-on approach to crafting each batch of beer. Whether you're a seasoned beer enthusiast or new to the craft scene,

Boise Brewing's staff are passionate about sharing their knowledge and making your visit memorable.

Signature Beers

Boise Brewing takes pride in its diverse lineup of beers, each crafted with locally sourced ingredients and a dedication to quality. Among their flagship offerings is the Broad Street Blonde, a crisp and refreshing ale that serves as a perfect introduction to their range. For those craving something more robust, the Down Down Extra Pale Ale delivers a hop-forward experience balanced by a smooth malt backbone.

The brewery's seasonal and limited-edition releases showcase the creativity and innovation of Boise Brewing's brewers. From the rich and velvety Black Cliffs American Stout to the citrusy and tropical flavors of the Hip Check IPA, each beer tells a story of craftsmanship and passion.

Taproom Experience

The taproom at Boise Brewing is more than just a place to enjoy great beer; it's a hub of community activity. Locals gather here after work to unwind, friends meet to catch up over a pint, and visitors from out of town discover the warmth and hospitality that defines Boise's spirit. The space features communal tables where conversations flow freely, as well as cozy nooks for those seeking a quieter moment.

Visitors can choose from a rotating selection of beers on tap, served fresh from the brewery's taps. The friendly and knowledgeable staff are always ready to offer recommendations based on your taste preferences or provide insights into the brewing process. Whether you prefer a flight of samples to explore different styles or a pint of your favorite brew, the taproom experience at Boise Brewing is designed to cater to every palate.

Events and Community Engagement

Boise Brewing's commitment to community extends beyond their brewing operations. Throughout the year, the brewery hosts a variety of events that bring people together and support local causes. From live music performances that fill the taproom with rhythm and energy to beer release parties that celebrate new creations, there's always something happening at Boise Brewing.

One of the brewery's standout initiatives is their "Pints for a Purpose" program, where selected beers are dedicated to raising funds for nonprofit organizations. By enjoying a pint of these special releases, patrons contribute to causes that benefit the Boise community, fostering a sense of connection and support among beer enthusiasts and philanthropists alike.

Visiting Tips

When planning your visit to Boise Brewing, here are a few tips to enhance your experience:

Hours: Check Boise Brewing's website or social media channels for their current operating hours, as they may vary seasonally or during special events.

Tours: While Boise Brewing does not offer formal brewery tours, guests can observe the brewing process from the taproom and chat with staff about their craft.

Food Options: While Boise Brewing does not have a kitchen, they often host food trucks outside the taproom, offering a variety of delicious options to complement your beer.

Merchandise: Don't forget to browse Boise Brewing's merchandise selection, which includes branded apparel, glassware, and other souvenirs perfect for beer enthusiasts.

Chapter 5: Day Trips and Beyond

Snake River Valley Wine Region: Wine Tastings and Scenic Drives

Exploring the Terroir and Climate

The Snake River Valley AVA benefits from a unique microclimate that contributes to the quality and diversity of its wines. Situated at high altitudes ranging from 2,000 to 3,000 feet above sea level, the region experiences warm summers, cool evenings, and a significant diurnal temperature variation—ideal conditions for grape cultivation. The volcanic soils, mixed with sedimentary deposits from ancient glacial Lake Idaho, impart distinctive mineral characteristics to the wines grown here.

Top Wineries and Vineyards

Bitner Vineyards

Address: 16645 Plum Rd, Caldwell, ID 83607

Tucked away in the heart of the Snake River Valley, Bitner Vineyards is a family-owned estate renowned for its sustainable farming practices and artisanal wines. Visitors can enjoy guided tours of the vineyards, where varietals such as Syrah, Merlot, and Viognier thrive in the volcanic soils. The tasting room offers panoramic views of the Owyhee Mountains, providing a serene backdrop for sampling Bitner's acclaimed vintages.

Ste. Chapelle Winery

Address: 19348 Lowell Rd, Caldwell, ID 83607

As Idaho's largest and most historic winery, Ste. Chapelle Winery is a cornerstone of the Snake River Valley wine scene. Established in 1976, it has garnered a reputation for producing premium wines that capture the essence of the region. Visitors can tour the state-of-the-art facilities, including the expansive barrel room and the picturesque vineyards, followed by tastings of their award-winning Riesling, Chardonnay, and Cabernet Sauvignon.

Sawtooth Winery

Address: 13750 Surrey Ln, Nampa, ID 83686

Situated on a sun-drenched slope overlooking the Snake River, Sawtooth Winery combines breathtaking views with exceptional wines crafted from locally sourced grapes. The estate specializes in cool-climate varietals like Pinot Gris and Tempranillo, reflecting the region's commitment to sustainable viticulture. Visitors can participate in guided tours of the production facilities and enjoy tastings in the rustic-chic tasting room or on the outdoor patio.

Koenig Vineyards

Address: 21452 Hoskins Rd, Caldwell, ID 83607

Koenig Vineyards is celebrated for its handcrafted wines that showcase the distinctiveness of Idaho's Snake River Valley. The estate's vineyards, planted with varieties such as Malbec and Petit Verdot, benefit from the region's rich volcanic soils and abundant sunshine. Wine enthusiasts can explore the state-of-the-art winemaking facilities and sample Koenig's acclaimed Reserve Merlot and Ice Wine, accompanied by stunning views of the surrounding countryside.

Scenic Drives and Vineyard Trails

Exploring the Snake River Valley Wine Region isn't just about tasting exceptional wines—it's also about soaking in the breathtaking scenery that surrounds the vineyards. Several scenic drives offer a leisurely way to experience the beauty of this AVA:

Sunset Wine Trail: Follow this picturesque route as the sun sets over the vine-covered hills, starting from Caldwell and winding through some of the region's most acclaimed wineries.

Snake River Scenic Byway: This iconic drive traces the path of the Snake River, offering panoramic views of the valley and opportunities to stop at wineries like Bitner Vineyards and Sawtooth Winery along the way.

Owyhee Uplands Backcountry Byway: For adventurous travelers, this rugged route showcases the dramatic landscapes of the Owyhee Mountains and provides access to remote vineyards like Huston Vineyards, known for their bold red blends.

Wine Tasting Tips and Recommendations

Plan Ahead: Many wineries in the Snake River Valley require reservations for tastings, especially during peak seasons. It's advisable to check each winery's website or call ahead to secure your spot.

Designated Driver: If you plan to visit multiple wineries in a day, designate a driver or consider booking a guided tour to ensure a safe and enjoyable experience.

Explore Beyond Wine: Some wineries offer additional experiences such as vineyard tours, food pairings, and seasonal events. Take advantage of these opportunities to deepen your understanding of Idaho's winemaking traditions.

Sun Valley Resort: Skiing, Golf, and Year-Round Recreation

Overview of Sun Valley Resort

Founded in 1936 by W. Averell Harriman, Sun Valley Resort holds the distinction of being America's first destination ski resort. Located just over 150 miles from Boise, it has long been a favored retreat for celebrities, athletes, and families seeking both adventure and relaxation in a breathtaking natural setting.

Winter Wonderland: Skiing and Snowboarding

Ski Terrain and Trails

Sun Valley boasts over 2,000 acres of skiable terrain spread across Bald Mountain (Baldy) and Dollar Mountain, catering to skiers and snowboarders of all skill levels. Baldy, the main draw, features 13 chairlifts and 65 named runs, offering everything from gentle groomers to challenging steeps. Dollar Mountain, ideal for beginners and families, offers gentle slopes and a terrain park for freestyle enthusiasts.

Signature Runs and Highlights

Warm Springs: Known for its steep pitches and challenging moguls, ideal for advanced skiers seeking thrills.

Christmas Bowl: Offers powder-filled glades and a backcountry-like experience with stunning views of the surrounding mountains.

Seattle Ridge: A mix of intermediate and advanced runs with excellent tree skiing opportunities and breathtaking panoramas.

Ski School and Instruction

Sun Valley Ski School provides personalized instruction for skiers and snowboarders of all ages and abilities. Private lessons and group clinics are available, focusing on technique enhancement, safety, and enjoyment of the mountain terrain.

Après-Ski and Dining

After a day on the slopes, visitors can unwind at one of Sun Valley's cozy lodges or explore the vibrant après-ski scene in nearby Ketchum. From fine dining at the renowned Roundhouse Restaurant atop Baldy to casual bites at River Run Lodge, there's something to satisfy every palate.

Summer Splendor: Golf and Outdoor Activities

Championship Golf Courses

Sun Valley boasts two championship golf courses that beckon golfers with their scenic layouts and challenging fairways:

Trail Creek Golf Course: Designed by Robert Trent Jones Jr., this 18-hole course winds through the Wood River Valley, offering stunning views and a challenging game for golfers of all levels.

White Clouds Golf Course: A 9-hole, par-3 course designed by Don Knott, perfect for a quick round or family outing amidst panoramic mountain views.

Outdoor Pursuits

Beyond golf, Sun Valley transforms into a playground for outdoor enthusiasts during the summer months:

Hiking and Mountain Biking: Explore over 400 miles of trails that crisscross the Sawtooth National Recreation Area, ranging from leisurely nature walks to challenging alpine ascents.

Fly Fishing: Cast a line in the pristine waters of the Big Wood River or Silver Creek, renowned for their abundant trout populations and serene surroundings.

Horseback Riding: Experience the beauty of Idaho's backcountry on horseback with guided trail rides and pack trips offered by local outfitters.

Year-Round Resort Amenities and Attractions

Sun Valley Lodge and Accommodations

The historic Sun Valley Lodge, a centerpiece of the resort, offers luxury accommodations with a blend of rustic charm and modern amenities. Guests can relax in elegantly appointed rooms and suites, enjoy world-class dining, and rejuvenate at the luxurious spa.

Shopping and Entertainment

Explore the Sun Valley Village for boutique shopping, art galleries, and live entertainment throughout the year. From local crafts to upscale fashion, the village offers a diverse shopping experience complemented by cultural events and outdoor concerts.

Special Events and Festivals

Sun Valley hosts a variety of seasonal events and festivals that showcase the region's culture, music, and culinary delights. From the Sun Valley Film Festival to the Sun Valley Writers' Conference, there's always something happening to enrich your visit.

Getting There and Practical Information

Directions from Boise

Sun Valley Resort is approximately a 2.5 to 3-hour drive from Boise, accessible via US-20 and ID-75. Rental cars, shuttles, and private transportation services are available for travelers looking to explore the scenic drive through Idaho's countryside.

Lodging and Accommodations

In addition to the Sun Valley Lodge, visitors can choose from a range of accommodations including cozy mountain lodges, condominium rentals, and vacation homes nestled within the resort and surrounding areas.

Weather and Climate

Sun Valley experiences a continental climate with cold winters and warm summers. Snowfall typically begins in

November and lasts through March, making it an ideal destination for winter sports enthusiasts. Summers are mild and pleasant, perfect for outdoor activities and exploring the natural beauty of the region.

Shoshone Falls: The "Niagara of the West" in Twin Falls

Discovering Shoshone Falls

Located approximately five miles east of the city of Twin Falls, Shoshone Falls is easily accessible via Shoshone Falls Park Road, which leads directly to the park entrance. As you approach the falls, the roar of the water and the mist in the air announce your arrival to this natural marvel.

The Magnificent Cascade

Standing at 212 feet tall—higher than Niagara Falls—Shoshone Falls is one of the largest natural waterfalls in the United States by volume, particularly impressive during the spring snowmelt when water levels are at their peak. The falls are fed by the Snake River, which carves its way through the Snake River Canyon, creating a spectacular display of power and beauty.

Best Times to Visit

The best time to visit Shoshone Falls depends largely on the flow of the Snake River, which can vary throughout the year. Generally, the spring months, especially April and May, offer the highest water levels due to snowmelt from the surrounding mountains. During this time, the falls are at their most dramatic, with a thunderous rush of water cascading over the cliffs.

Exploring Shoshone Falls Park

Shoshone Falls Park provides excellent vantage points for viewing the falls from various angles. The park features well-maintained pathways and viewing platforms that offer panoramic views of the falls and the Snake River Canyon. Visitors can take leisurely walks along the trails, stopping at designated viewpoints to photograph the falls and take in the awe-inspiring scenery.

Activities and Recreation

Beyond sightseeing, Shoshone Falls Park offers opportunities for outdoor recreation and relaxation. Picnic areas with tables and grills are available, making it a perfect spot for a family outing or a scenic lunch overlooking the falls. Hiking enthusiasts can explore nearby trails that wind through the canyon, offering glimpses of the Snake River and its rugged landscape.

Photography Tips

For photographers, Shoshone Falls presents a myriad of opportunities to capture stunning images. The morning and late afternoon light casts a warm glow on the falls, enhancing their natural beauty. Consider bringing a tripod to capture long exposure shots of the cascading water, or experiment with different angles to showcase the scale and power of the falls against the backdrop of the canyon.

Wildlife and Natural Habitat

The area surrounding Shoshone Falls is rich in wildlife and natural habitat. Keep an eye out for native bird species such as bald eagles and osprey, which can often be seen soaring above the canyon or fishing in the river below. Binoculars are recommended for birdwatching enthusiasts looking to spot these majestic creatures in their natural environment.

Nearby Attractions

While visiting Shoshone Falls, consider exploring other nearby attractions in the Twin Falls area. Perrine Bridge, spanning the Snake River Canyon, offers breathtaking views and is a popular spot for base jumping and scenic drives.

Snake River Canyon Rim Trail provides opportunities for hiking and biking, with panoramic vistas of the canyon and the Snake River below.

Practical Information

Address: Shoshone Falls Park, 4155 Shoshone Falls Grade, Twin Falls, ID 83301

Hours: The park is open year-round from dawn to dusk. Entrance fees may apply during peak visitor seasons.

Facilities: Restrooms, picnic areas, and parking facilities are available within the park. Accessibility options are provided for visitors with disabilities.

Safety: Pay attention to safety guidelines and signage while exploring the park, especially near the canyon edges and waterfalls. Swimming and climbing on the rocks are prohibited due to safety concerns and strong currents in the river.

Chapter 6: Events and Festivals

Treefort Music Fest: Indie Music and Community Vibes

History and Evolution

Treefort Music Fest emerged from Boise's rich artistic community, born out of a desire to showcase local talent and create a platform for independent artists. Founded by a group of passionate individuals, including Eric Gilbert, Drew Lorona, and Lori Shandro Outen, the festival quickly gained momentum, blending diverse musical genres with an inclusive and welcoming atmosphere.

Each year, Treefort expands its lineup and activities, embracing not only music but also art, film, comedy, and technology. What started as a grassroots gathering has evolved into a nationally recognized event, attracting thousands of attendees and becoming a highlight on Boise's cultural calendar.

Music Lineup and Venues

Treefort Music Fest boasts a lineup that spans genres, from indie rock and folk to electronic and experimental sounds. The festival curates over 400 bands across numerous venues, ensuring there's something for every musical taste. Venues range from intimate bars and clubs to outdoor stages and historic theaters, creating a dynamic tapestry of performances throughout downtown Boise.

Key Venues:

Main Stage at Boise Basque Block

Address: 601 Grove St, Boise, ID 83702

Located at the heart of the festival grounds, the Main Stage at Boise Basque Block hosts headline acts and larger performances, offering a central hub for festival-goers to gather and enjoy music under the open sky.

Neurolux

Address: 111 N 11th St, Boise, ID 83702

Known for its intimate atmosphere and stellar sound quality, Neurolux is a favorite among Treefort attendees. This venue showcases both emerging artists and established acts, providing a cozy setting for memorable performances.

El Korah Shrine

Address: 1118 W Idaho St, Boise, ID 83702

A historic venue with ornate architecture, El Korah Shrine offers a unique backdrop for Treefort performances. Attendees can experience music in a setting that blends cultural heritage with contemporary creativity.

The Olympic

Address: 1009 Main St, Boise, ID 83702

As one of Boise's premier live music venues, The Olympic plays host to Treefort bands throughout the festival. Its vibrant atmosphere and central location make it a hotspot for discovering new music and enjoying energetic performances.

Art and Innovation

Beyond music, Treefort Music Fest embraces art and innovation, enriching the festival experience with visual installations, interactive exhibits, and workshops. Local artists contribute murals and sculptures that transform Boise's streets into a vibrant outdoor gallery. Attendees can also participate in panels and discussions on topics ranging from music industry trends to creative entrepreneurship, fostering dialogue and collaboration among artists and enthusiasts alike.

Community Engagement

At its core, Treefort Music Fest is about community. The festival collaborates with local businesses, nonprofits, and volunteers to create an inclusive and sustainable event. Attendees are encouraged to explore Boise's neighborhoods, support local establishments, and immerse themselves in the city's culture beyond the festival grounds. From neighborhood block parties to pop-up markets showcasing handmade goods, Treefort fosters connections that extend far beyond the music.

Culinary Delights

Food plays a central role at Treefort Music Fest, with a diverse array of culinary offerings that reflect Boise's thriving dining scene. Food trucks line the streets, serving up everything from gourmet tacos to artisanal ice cream. Local breweries and wineries also join the festivities, offering craft beers and wines that complement the festival experience. Whether you're craving a quick bite between sets or looking to indulge in a leisurely meal, Treefort ensures that culinary delights are never far away.

Tips for Attendees

Tickets and Passes: Purchase tickets early, as Treefort Music Fest often sells out. Consider VIP passes for exclusive access and perks.

Accommodation: Book accommodations well in advance, as hotels and Airbnb options fill up quickly during the festival.

Transportation: Navigate Boise with ease using public transportation, rideshares, or bicycles. Parking downtown can be limited, so plan accordingly.

Stay Informed: Download the Treefort app for up-to-date schedules, venue maps, and notifications about lineup additions or changes.

Boise River Festival: Waterfront Celebrations and Family Fun

Overview

The Boise River Festival typically takes place over several days during the summer months, usually in late June or early July. It serves as a celebration of Boise's connection to the river and its role in the city's identity. The festival grounds span along the Boise River Greenbelt, a scenic pathway that winds through parks, gardens, and recreational areas, providing a picturesque backdrop for the event's activities.

Activities and Attractions

Waterfront Events: The festival's main draw is its array of waterfront events, which cater to all ages and interests. Families can enjoy river rafting and kayaking excursions, guided by experienced local outfitters who provide equipment and ensure safety on the water. These activities offer a thrilling way to experience the Boise River and are popular among both residents and tourists seeking outdoor adventure.

Location: Boise River Greenbelt, various access points along the river.

Live Music and Performances: Throughout the festival, live music and performances can be found at multiple stages set up along the riverbank. Local bands, as well as regional and national acts, entertain crowds with a mix of genres from folk and rock to jazz and blues. Families often spread out picnic blankets on the grassy banks, enjoying the music while taking in views of the river.

Locations: Main stage near Ann Morrison Park, additional stages at Esther Simplot Park and Julia Davis Park.

Arts and Crafts: Artisans and craft vendors line the festival grounds, offering handmade goods ranging from jewelry and pottery to paintings and photography. Visitors can browse unique creations, meet the artists, and purchase souvenirs that reflect Boise's artistic community and culture.

Locations: Vendor booths throughout the festival area, particularly concentrated near Julia Davis Park.

Carnival Rides and Games: A carnival atmosphere permeates the festival with rides, games, and activities designed for children and families. From classic carnival games like ring toss and duck pond to thrilling rides such as ferris wheels and bumper cars, there's no shortage of entertainment options to delight festival-goers of all ages.

Locations: Carnival area near Ann Morrison Park.

Food and Drink: A diverse selection of food vendors offers everything from local specialties like Idaho potatoes and Basque cuisine to international flavors and festival favorites like funnel cakes and corn dogs. Beverage tents provide refreshments ranging from craft beer and local wines to refreshing lemonades and smoothies, ensuring that visitors stay hydrated and satisfied throughout the festivities.

Locations: Food courts scattered throughout the festival grounds, with concentrated areas near main stages and along the Greenbelt.

Family Activities: The Boise River Festival prides itself on being family-friendly, offering interactive activities and educational exhibits geared toward children and parents. From wildlife demonstrations and science experiments to storytelling sessions and arts workshops, these activities aim to engage young minds and foster a sense of community among attendees.

Locations: Family activity zones near Esther Simplot Park and Boise Zoo.

Special Highlights

Fireworks Spectacular: One of the most anticipated events of the Boise River Festival is the fireworks display that lights up the night sky over the Boise River. This grand finale typically takes place on the festival's closing night and draws crowds from across the region who gather along the riverbanks to witness the dazzling show of colors and patterns.

Location: Best viewing spots along the Boise River Greenbelt, particularly near Ann Morrison Park and Julia Davis Park.

Community Partnerships and Sponsorships: The festival's success is due in part to the support of local businesses, organizations, and volunteers who contribute their time, resources, and expertise to ensure a memorable experience for all participants. Community partnerships enhance the festival's offerings, from eco-friendly initiatives to accessibility accommodations that make the event inclusive for everyone.

Acknowledgments: Major sponsors are recognized on festival signage, programs, and promotional materials, showcasing their commitment to Boise's cultural and recreational community.

Visitor Tips and Logistics

Parking and Transportation: Limited parking is available near festival grounds, so visitors are encouraged to use public transportation, bike, or walk via the Boise River Greenbelt to access the event. Shuttle services may be provided from designated parking areas to alleviate congestion during peak times.

Public Transit: Valley Regional Transit (VRT) offers bus routes that connect downtown Boise with festival locations, providing a convenient and environmentally friendly transportation option.

Weather Preparedness: Boise's summer weather can be warm and sunny, so attendees should dress comfortably and bring sunscreen, hats, and sunglasses to protect against UV rays. Light layers are recommended for cooler evenings, especially during the fireworks display.

Accessibility: The festival strives to be accessible to individuals of all abilities, with designated accessible parking, ADA-compliant facilities, and accommodations for sensory sensitivities upon request. Volunteers and staff are available to assist visitors with any additional needs or inquiries.

Boise Farmers Market: Fresh Produce and Local Goods Galore

Overview of the Boise Farmers Market

Located at 10th and Grove Streets, just a stone's throw from the bustling downtown core, the Boise Farmers Market operates from April through December, providing a seasonal feast for the senses every Saturday morning from 9:00 AM to 1:00 PM. This open-air market is not just a place to shop—it's a community hub where farmers, artisans, and local producers converge to share their passion for quality, sustainable products.

What to Expect

As you approach the market, the vibrant colors of fresh fruits and vegetables beckon, along with the tantalizing aromas of freshly baked bread, artisanal cheeses, and brewed coffee. The market is divided into sections, each offering its own unique charm and variety:

1. Fresh Produce Stands

Start your journey at the heart of the market—the produce stands. Here, local farmers proudly display their seasonal harvests, from heirloom tomatoes and crisp salad greens to juicy peaches and Idaho's famous potatoes. Expect to find organic options and specialty crops that reflect the region's agricultural diversity.

Address: Boise Farmers Market, 10th and Grove Streets, Boise, ID 83702

2. Artisanal Foods and Beverages

Adjacent to the produce stands, you'll discover a treasure trove of artisanal foods crafted with care. Indulge in handcrafted cheeses from local creameries, sample small-batch preserves made from Idaho-grown fruits, or pick up a loaf of freshly baked bread still warm from the oven. Don't miss the opportunity to taste locally roasted coffee and specialty teas that highlight Idaho's burgeoning craft beverage scene.

Address: Boise Farmers Market, 10th and Grove Streets, Boise, ID 83702

3. Local Crafts and Art

Beyond food, the market showcases the creativity of Idaho's artisans. Browse through stalls featuring handmade pottery, jewelry crafted from local gemstones, and original artwork that reflects the natural beauty of the Gem State. It's the perfect place to find unique gifts or mementos that capture the spirit of Boise.

Address: Boise Farmers Market, 10th and Grove Streets, Boise, ID 83702

4. Prepared Foods and Ready-to-Eat Delights

Hungry shoppers can satisfy their cravings with an array of ready-to-eat offerings. From gourmet crepes and wood-fired pizzas to savory tamales and freshly grilled kabobs, the market vendors serve up a diverse menu of culinary delights. Grab a seat at one of the communal tables and savor your meal amidst the lively market ambiance.

Address: Boise Farmers Market, 10th and Grove Streets, Boise, ID 83702

5. Community and Events

The Boise Farmers Market is more than a marketplace—it's a gathering place for the community. Throughout the season, visitors can enjoy live music performances by local artists, cooking demonstrations featuring seasonal ingredients, and educational workshops on topics ranging from organic gardening to sustainable farming practices. Check the market's website or social media channels for upcoming events and special activities.

Address: Boise Farmers Market, 10th and Grove Streets, Boise, ID 83702

Insider Tips for Visiting the Boise Farmers Market

Arrive Early: To beat the crowds and snag the freshest produce, plan to arrive when the market opens at 9:00 AM.

Bring Cash: While some vendors may accept cards, cash is often preferred and ensures smooth transactions.

BYOB (Bring Your Own Bag): Help reduce waste by bringing your own reusable bags or baskets for shopping.

Parking: Limited street parking is available nearby, but consider carpooling, biking, or using public transportation to ease parking woes.

Chapter 7: Insider Tips and Recommendations

Local Favorites: Hidden Gems and Must-Try Experiences

1. Rediscover Downtown Boise: Historic Charm and Modern Delights

Address: Downtown Boise, Boise, ID 83702

Description: Downtown Boise is the heart of the city, blending historic architecture with modern attractions. Start your exploration at the intersection of Capitol Boulevard and Main Street, where you'll find the iconic Boise Centre and nearby Boise City Hall. Wander down bustling streets lined with shops, cafes, and local boutiques, or take a leisurely stroll along the Boise River Greenbelt, just a stone's throw away.

Must-Visit Highlights:

Freak Alley Gallery: Located between Bannock and Idaho Streets, Freak Alley Gallery is an ever-evolving outdoor art gallery featuring vibrant murals and graffiti art by local and international artists.

Idaho State Capitol: Explore Idaho's political history with a guided tour of the Idaho State Capitol building, showcasing stunning architecture and historical artifacts. Located at 700 W Jefferson St, Boise, ID 83720.

Local Tip: For a taste of local flavors, visit the Capital City Public Market on Saturdays, where you can sample fresh produce, artisanal goods, and food trucks from around the region.

2. Hyde Park: A Quaint Neighborhood Retreat

Address: N 13th St & E Hyde Park, Boise, ID 83702

Description: Tucked away in Boise's North End, Hyde Park exudes a small-town charm with tree-lined streets and historic architecture. This neighborhood is a favorite among locals for its cozy cafes, boutique shops, and relaxed atmosphere.

Must-Visit Highlights:

Camel's Back Park: A popular spot for outdoor enthusiasts, Camel's Back Park offers hiking trails, picnic areas, and panoramic views of the city skyline from its foothill location.

Goody's Soda Fountain & Candy Store: Step back in time at this nostalgic soda fountain, serving up handmade ice cream, old-fashioned sodas, and a wide selection of candies. Located at 1502 N 13th St, Boise, ID 83702.

Local Tip: Don't miss the Hyde Park Street Fair held annually in September, featuring local artists, live music, and family-friendly activities.

3. Boise Bench: Scenic Views and Local Flavor

Address: Boise Bench, Boise, ID 83705

Description: South of downtown lies the Boise Bench, an elevated plateau offering stunning views of the city and the surrounding mountains. Known for its residential neighborhoods and diverse dining options, the Boise Bench provides a glimpse into local life away from the city center.

Must-Visit Highlights:

Drive the Boise Rim: Take a scenic drive along the Boise Rim, accessible from multiple points including Owyhee Street, to enjoy panoramic views of the city and the Boise River below.

Lucky 13: A beloved local burger joint known for its gourmet burgers, craft beers, and laid-back atmosphere. Located at 3662 S Eckert Rd, Boise, ID 83716.

Local Tip: Visit during sunset for breathtaking views and capture the city lights as they come to life.

4. Boise River Recreation: Serenity in Nature

Address: Boise River, Boise, ID 83702

Description: The Boise River is a central feature of the city, offering both recreational opportunities and a serene escape into nature. Whether you prefer kayaking along its gentle waters, cycling along the scenic Greenbelt, or simply relaxing by its banks, the river provides a refreshing respite from urban life.

Must-Visit Highlights:

Boise River Greenbelt: Stretching over 25 miles, the Greenbelt is a pedestrian and cycling path that winds along the Boise River, passing through parks, wildlife habitats, and scenic overlooks.

Barber Park: A gateway to the Boise River, offering river access for tubing, picnicking areas, and a starting point for float trips downstream. Located at 4049 S Eckert Rd, Boise, ID 83716.

Local Tip: Rent a paddleboard or kayak from local outfitters for a leisurely float down the river during the warmer months.

5. Basque Block: Cultural Heritage and Culinary Delights

Address: W Grove St, Boise, ID 83702

Description: Immerse yourself in Boise's Basque heritage at the Basque Block, a cultural hub where traditions thrive through food, festivals, and community gatherings. This vibrant neighborhood celebrates Boise's strong ties to Basque culture, dating back over a century.

Must-Visit Highlights:

Basque Museum & Cultural Center: Explore exhibits detailing the history and contributions of Basque immigrants to Idaho, including artifacts, photographs, and interactive displays. Located at 611 W Grove St, Boise, ID 83702.

Bar Gernika: A local favorite serving authentic Basque cuisine, including chorizo sandwiches, croquetas, and kalimotxos (red wine and cola). Located at 202 S Capitol Blvd, Boise, ID 83702.

Local Tip: Visit during the Jaialdi International Basque Festival held every five years, featuring dance performances, traditional sports, and Basque music.

6. Boise Art Scene: Galleries and Cultural Hotspots

Address: Various locations throughout Boise

Description: Boise's art scene is thriving, with galleries, studios, and public art installations scattered throughout the city. From contemporary works to local creations, the art community in Boise offers a diverse range of experiences for art enthusiasts and casual visitors alike.

Must-Visit Highlights:

Boise Art Museum (BAM): Featuring rotating exhibits of contemporary art, ceramics, and sculpture, BAM is a cultural centerpiece in Boise's art scene. Located at 670 Julia Davis Dr, Boise, ID 83702.

Freak Alley Gallery: An ever-evolving outdoor gallery showcasing colorful murals and graffiti art by local and international artists. Located between Bannock and Idaho Streets, Boise, ID 83702.

Local Tip: Explore during First Thursday events, when galleries and studios open their doors to the public for art walks, live music, and meet-the-artist receptions.

7. Local Breweries and Taprooms: Craft Beer Culture

Address: Various locations throughout Boise

Description: Boise's craft beer scene has exploded in recent years, with breweries and taprooms offering a wide range of locally brewed beers, ciders, and meads. Whether you're a beer aficionado or new to the scene, Boise's breweries promise a taste of local flavor and community spirit.

Must-Visit Highlights:

Payette Brewing Company: Known for its year-round and seasonal brews, Payette Brewing Company offers a spacious taproom with outdoor seating and brewery tours. Located at 733 S Pioneer St, Boise, ID 83702.

Woodland Empire Ale Craft: A small-batch brewery focusing on experimental and barrel-aged beers, with a cozy taproom featuring rotating taps and local art displays. Located at 1114 W Front St, Boise, ID 83702.

Local Tip: Check out Boise Ale Trail, a self-guided tour showcasing the city's best breweries and earning rewards along the way for visiting participating locations.

8. North End Neighborhood: Quaint Cafes and Local Flavor

Address: North End, Boise, ID 83702

Description: Known for its tree-lined streets, historic homes, and community-focused atmosphere, Boise's North End is a charming neighborhood brimming with character. From cozy cafes to local shops, the North End invites visitors to explore its unique blend of old-world charm and modern conveniences.

Must-Visit Highlights:

Java: A local coffeehouse chain with multiple locations in the North End, offering artisanal coffee, homemade pastries, and a welcoming atmosphere. Located at 223 N 6th St, Boise, ID 83702.

Goody's Soda Fountain & Candy Store: A nostalgic soda fountain serving handmade ice cream, old-fashioned sodas, and an extensive selection of candies. Located at 1502 N 13th St, Boise, ID 83702.

Local Tip: Visit during the Hyde Park Street Fair held annually in September, featuring local artists, live music, and community gatherings.

9. Boise's Culinary Scene: Farm-to-Table Dining

Address: Various locations throughout Boise

Description: Boise's culinary landscape is a reflection of its diverse community, offering everything from farm-to-table dining experiences to international flavors and innovative dishes. Whether you're craving comfort food or gourmet cuisine, Boise's restaurants and eateries deliver flavors that celebrate local ingredients and global influences.

Must-Visit Highlights:

The Fork: A farm-to-table restaurant focusing on locally sourced ingredients, seasonal menus, and a welcoming ambiance. Located at 199 N 8th St, Boise, ID 83702.

State & Lemp: A culinary destination offering multi-course tasting menus that showcase Idaho's bounty and creative culinary techniques. Located at 2870 W State St, Boise, ID 83702.

Local Tip: Explore the Boise Farmers Market on Saturdays for fresh produce, artisanal goods, and food trucks offering a taste of Boise's culinary diversity.

10. Outdoor Adventures: Explore Beyond Boise

Address: Various locations surrounding Boise

Description: Beyond the city limits, Boise's surrounding areas offer outdoor adventures and natural wonders waiting to be explored. From hiking in the Boise National Forest to exploring the Snake River Valley wine region, outdoor enthusiasts will find endless opportunities to connect with nature and discover hidden gems.

Must-Visit Highlights:

Boise National Forest: A vast wilderness area offering hiking trails, camping sites, and scenic drives through forests of pine and fir trees. Located northeast of Boise, accessible via State Hwy 21.

Snake River Valley Wine Region: Discover Idaho's burgeoning wine scene with tastings at local wineries and vineyards, offering scenic views and award-winning wines. Located west of Boise, accessible via I-84 and US-20.

Local Tip: Plan a day trip to Lucky Peak State Park for boating, fishing, and picnicking along the shores of Lucky Peak Reservoir, just a short drive from downtown Boise.

Budget-Friendly Boise: Free and Low-Cost Activities

Outdoor Adventures and Scenic Spots

Boise is renowned for its stunning natural beauty and outdoor recreational opportunities. Whether you're an avid hiker, nature enthusiast, or simply enjoy a peaceful stroll, these spots are perfect for enjoying Boise's landscapes without spending a dime.

1. Boise River Greenbelt

Location: Runs along the Boise River through downtown Boise

Description: Stretching over 25 miles, the Boise River Greenbelt offers a scenic pathway for walkers, joggers, and cyclists. Enjoy views of the river, lush greenery, and occasional wildlife sightings. Access points include Julia Davis Park, Ann Morrison Park, and Boise State University.

2. Kathryn Albertson Park

Location: 1001 Americana Blvd, Boise, ID 83706

Description: This 41-acre park features a tranquil pond, walking paths, and a variety of native flora and fauna. Perfect for birdwatching or a leisurely picnic, Kathryn Albertson Park provides a serene escape in the heart of Boise.

3. Boise Foothills

Location: Access points throughout Boise, including Camel's Back Park and Hulls Gulch Reserve

Description: Explore miles of hiking and biking trails in the Boise Foothills, offering panoramic views of the city and surrounding mountains. Popular trails include the Hulls Gulch Interpretive Trail and the Camel's Back Park Trailhead.

Cultural and Historical Exploration

Delve into Boise's rich history and vibrant cultural scene with these budget-friendly options, ranging from museums to historic landmarks.

4. Idaho State Capitol

Location: 700 W Jefferson St, Boise, ID 83702

Description: Take a free guided tour of the Idaho State Capitol, an architectural masterpiece showcasing Idaho's political history. Marvel at the rotunda, legislative chambers, and historical artifacts on display.

5. Basque Block

Location: Grove St between Capitol Blvd and 6th St, Boise, ID 83702

Description: Immerse yourself in Boise's Basque heritage with a stroll through the Basque Block. Visit the Basque Museum & Cultural Center (admission fees may apply) and explore the Basque Market for authentic cuisine and cultural insights.

6. Freak Alley Gallery

Location: 210 N 9th St, Boise, ID 83702

Description: Discover one of Boise's most unique attractions at Freak Alley Gallery, an outdoor urban art gallery featuring vibrant murals and graffiti art. Admission is free, and the artwork changes regularly, providing a dynamic cultural experience.

Educational and Family-Friendly Activities

Boise offers several educational and family-friendly attractions that won't strain your budget, perfect for a day of learning and fun.

7. Discovery Center of Idaho

Location: 131 W Myrtle St, Boise, ID 83702

Description: While admission fees apply, the Discovery Center of Idaho occasionally offers free or discounted days. Explore interactive exhibits on science, technology, and innovation, ideal for children and curious minds alike.

8. Idaho Botanical Garden

Location: 2355 N Old Penitentiary Rd, Boise, ID 83712

Description: Enjoy free admission to the Idaho Botanical Garden on select days or during specific events. Discover themed gardens, seasonal blooms, and educational programs amidst the tranquil setting of the Old Idaho State Penitentiary.

Local Markets and Festivals

Experience Boise's vibrant community spirit through local markets, festivals, and events that celebrate art, culture, and culinary delights.

9. Capital City Public Market

Location: Downtown Boise, along 8th St between Bannock St and Main St

Description: Browse the Capital City Public Market, Boise's premier farmers' market featuring local produce, artisan crafts, and gourmet foods. Enjoy live music and a lively atmosphere every Saturday morning (seasonal, check schedule).

10. Alive After Five

Location: The Grove Plaza, 850 W Front St, Boise, ID 83702

Description: Join the community at Alive After Five, a free summer concert series held every Wednesday evening in downtown Boise. Enjoy live music, food vendors, and a festive ambiance.

Seasonal and Special Events

From seasonal celebrations to annual events, Boise hosts a variety of activities throughout the year that cater to diverse interests and budgets.

11. Treefort Music Fest

Location: Various venues throughout downtown Boise

Description: While Treefort Music Fest primarily requires tickets for entry, the festival offers numerous free events, including local music showcases, film screenings, and art installations. Experience Boise's indie music scene and community spirit during this multi-day event.

12. Shakespeare Festival

Location: Idaho Shakespeare Festival Amphitheater, 5657 Warm Springs Ave, Boise, ID 83716

Description: Enjoy free performances during the Idaho Shakespeare Festival's "Shakespeare in the Park" series. Pack a picnic and experience classic plays under the stars at the scenic amphitheater (seasonal, check schedule).

Practical Tips for Budget Travelers

Make the most of your budget-friendly Boise adventure with these practical tips and resources:

Free Admission Days: Many museums and attractions offer free admission days or discounted rates, so plan your visit accordingly.

Local Libraries: Visit Boise's public libraries for free Wi-Fi, reading areas, and occasional community events.

Walking Tours: Explore downtown Boise on foot with self-guided walking tours available online or through visitor information centers.

Public Transportation: Utilize Boise's affordable bus system (ValleyRide) for exploring the city and reaching nearby attractions.

Planning Your Visit: Practical Tips for a Seamless Trip

Understanding Boise: A Snapshot

Boise, the capital city of Idaho, sits in the southwestern part of the state, nestled along the Boise River and surrounded by the Boise Foothills to the northeast. It's known for its vibrant cultural scene, outdoor recreational opportunities, and a thriving local food and craft beer scene. The city combines its rich history with modern amenities, making it a popular destination for tourists and outdoor enthusiasts alike.

Getting There: Transportation Options

By Air:

Boise is served by the Boise Airport (BOI), located just a few miles south of downtown. The airport offers numerous daily flights from major cities across the United States, making it convenient to reach Boise from almost anywhere. Upon arrival, you can rent a car, take a taxi, or use ride-sharing services to get to your accommodation.

By Car:

If you're driving to Boise, major highways such as Interstate 84 connect the city with neighboring states like Oregon and Utah. Boise's central location in the state makes it a manageable drive from popular destinations within the region.

Public Transportation:

Boise's public transportation system, operated by Valley Regional Transit (VRT), includes buses that serve the city and surrounding areas. While not as extensive as some larger cities, the bus system provides a cost-effective way to navigate Boise if you prefer not to drive.

Best Times to Visit Boise

Boise experiences a semi-arid climate with hot summers and cold winters, influenced by its high desert location. The best times to visit depend largely on your preferences for weather and outdoor activities:

Spring (March to May): Spring brings mild temperatures and blooming wildflowers, making it an ideal time for outdoor adventures and exploring the city's parks and gardens.

Summer (June to August): Summer in Boise is hot and dry, with temperatures often reaching the 90s°F (30s°C). It's the perfect season for hiking, river activities, and attending outdoor festivals like the Boise River Festival and Alive After Five.

Fall (September to November): Fall offers cooler temperatures and vibrant foliage in the Boise Foothills. It's a great time for hiking, wine tasting in the nearby Snake River Valley, and attending cultural events.

Winter (December to February): Winter in Boise is cold, with occasional snowfall. While outdoor activities like skiing at Bogus Basin are popular, indoor attractions such as museums and theaters provide cozy options during colder days.

Where to Stay: Accommodation Options

Boise offers a variety of accommodation options to suit every traveler's preference and budget:

Downtown Boise:

Staying in downtown Boise puts you within walking distance of many attractions, restaurants, and nightlife options. Upscale hotels, boutique lodgings, and vacation rentals are all available downtown, offering convenience and proximity to the city's main sights.

North End:

The North End neighborhood offers a quieter, residential vibe with charming bed and breakfasts and guesthouses. It's ideal for travelers seeking a more relaxed atmosphere while still being close to downtown attractions.

Boise Bench:

Located south of downtown, the Boise Bench area provides affordable hotel chains and budget-friendly accommodations. It's a good option if you're looking to stay near the airport or have easy access to major highways.

East Boise:

East Boise, particularly around the Harris Ranch area, offers newer hotels and upscale accommodations. This area appeals to travelers seeking a quieter stay with easy access to outdoor activities along the Boise River Greenbelt.

Navigating Boise: Getting Around

Boise is a pedestrian-friendly city with bike lanes and sidewalks that make it easy to explore on foot. If you prefer to use public transportation or drive, here are some tips:

Public Transportation:

Valley Regional Transit (VRT) operates buses throughout Boise and its surrounding suburbs. The system is reliable for getting around downtown and nearby attractions, though schedules may vary on weekends and holidays.

Ride-Sharing Services:

Uber and Lyft operate in Boise, providing convenient options for traveling short distances or reaching destinations not easily accessible by public transit.

Car Rentals:

Renting a car in Boise is a popular choice for visitors wanting to explore beyond the city center. Major car rental companies have offices at the Boise Airport and downtown locations, offering a range of vehicles to suit your needs.

Biking:

Boise is known for its bike-friendly infrastructure, including the Boise River Greenbelt—a scenic pathway that stretches alongside the river. Many hotels offer bike rentals, and several bike shops in downtown Boise provide equipment and guided tours.

Must-See Attractions and Activities

Boise boasts a wealth of attractions and activities that showcase its natural beauty, cultural heritage, and community spirit:

Boise River Greenbelt:

This 25-mile pathway winds along the Boise River, offering picturesque views, parks, and access to outdoor activities such as biking, jogging, and picnicking. Don't miss the Idaho Anne Frank Human Rights Memorial and the Boise Zoo along the greenbelt.

Old Idaho Penitentiary:

Explore Boise's history at the Old Idaho Penitentiary, a former prison turned museum. Guided tours offer insights into prison life and infamous inmates who once called this place home.

Idaho State Capitol:

Visit the Idaho State Capitol building, an architectural gem located in downtown Boise. Guided tours provide access to the legislative chambers and historic artifacts, showcasing Idaho's political history.

Boise Art Museum:

Art enthusiasts will appreciate the Boise Art Museum's collection of contemporary art and rotating exhibitions. The museum hosts educational programs and events throughout the year, making it a cultural hub for locals and visitors alike.

Julia Davis Park:

Located near downtown Boise, Julia Davis Park is a sprawling green space with rose gardens, playgrounds, and several museums. Visit the Idaho Historical Museum, the Boise Art Museum, and the Discovery Center of Idaho—all within walking distance of each other.

Dining and Nightlife: Where to Eat and Drink

Boise's dining scene reflects its diverse community and commitment to local ingredients. From farm-to-table restaurants to international cuisine, here are some dining options to consider:

Fork:

Located in downtown Boise, Fork showcases Idaho's bounty with a menu focused on locally sourced ingredients. Try their famous Idaho trout or seasonal salads paired with local wines and craft beers.

Basque Market:

Experience Boise's Basque heritage at the Basque Market, where you can enjoy tapas, paella, and chorizo sandwiches. Don't miss their Friday night dinners with live music and traditional dancing.

10 Barrel Brewing Co.:

For craft beer enthusiasts, 10 Barrel Brewing Co. offers a relaxed atmosphere and a rotating selection of beers brewed on-site. Their rooftop patio provides stunning views of downtown Boise and the foothills beyond.

Bar Gernika:

Another nod to Boise's Basque community, Bar Gernika serves up traditional Basque dishes such as croquetas, chorizo sandwiches, and lamb stew. Pair your meal with a refreshing glass of Kalimotxo—a Basque cocktail made with red wine and cola.

Shopping in Boise: Local Finds and Souvenirs

Boise's shopping scene ranges from independent boutiques to local markets, offering unique finds and souvenirs:

Boise Farmers Market:

Open on Saturdays from April to October, the Boise Farmers Market showcases local produce, artisanal goods, and handmade crafts. It's a great place to sample Idaho's culinary delights and support local farmers and artisans.

Old Boise:

Explore the historic district of Old Boise, where you'll find eclectic shops, galleries, and cafes housed in beautifully preserved buildings. Look for locally made jewelry, pottery, and artwork as memorable souvenirs of your trip.

Boise Towne Square Mall:

For a more traditional shopping experience, visit Boise Towne Square Mall—a large shopping center with national retailers, restaurants, and entertainment options. It's conveniently located near major highways and offers ample parking.

Health and Safety Tips

Boise is generally a safe city for travelers, but it's always wise to take precautions to ensure a worry-free visit:

Stay Informed:

Check local news and weather updates before your trip, especially during winter months when road conditions can be affected by snow and ice.

Stay Hydrated:

Boise's high desert climate can lead to dry conditions, so it's important to drink plenty of water, especially if you plan to spend time outdoors.

Be Aware of Altitude:

Boise sits at an elevation of approximately 2,700 feet (823 meters) above sea level. If you're coming from lower altitudes, take it easy during your first day to acclimate to the altitude.

Emergency Services:

Know the emergency contact numbers for Boise, including police, fire, and medical services. In case of an emergency, dial 911 for immediate assistance.

Local Etiquette and Customs

Boiseans are known for their friendly demeanor and welcoming attitude towards visitors. To ensure a positive experience, consider these local customs:

Respect the Outdoors:

Boise residents take pride in their natural surroundings. Whether you're hiking in the foothills or picnicking along the river, remember to leave no trace and respect wildlife.

Support Local Businesses:

Boise has a strong community of local artisans, farmers, and entrepreneurs. Show your support by shopping at local markets, dining at independent restaurants, and visiting neighborhood boutiques.

Be Courteous on Trails and Pathways:

If you're biking or walking along the Boise River Greenbelt or hiking in the foothills, yield to pedestrians and follow trail etiquette to ensure everyone enjoys their outdoor experience.

Useful Contacts and Resources

1. Transportation

Boise Airport (BOI)

Address: 3201 Airport Way, Boise, ID 83705

Phone: (208) 383-3110

Website: iflyboise.com

Located just south of downtown Boise, Boise Airport serves as the primary gateway to the city and the surrounding region. It offers domestic and limited international flights, with various ground transportation options available, including rental cars, shuttles, and taxis.

Valley Regional Transit (VRT)

Address: 700 NE 2nd St, Meridian, ID 83642

Phone: (208) 345-7433

Website: valleyregionaltransit.org

VRT operates bus services throughout the Boise metropolitan area, providing convenient and affordable transportation options for getting around the city and neighboring communities.

Boise GreenBike

Website: boise.greenbike.com

Boise GreenBike offers a bike-sharing program with numerous stations conveniently located throughout downtown Boise. It's a great way to explore the city at your own pace while enjoying the scenic Boise River Greenbelt and other bike-friendly routes.

2. Medical Services

St. Luke's Boise Medical Center

Address: 190 E Bannock St, Boise, ID 83712

Phone: (208) 381-2222

Website: stlukesonline.org

St. Luke's Boise Medical Center is a leading healthcare facility in Boise, offering comprehensive medical services, emergency care, and specialized treatments. It's centrally located near downtown Boise for convenient access.

Saint Alphonsus Regional Medical Center

Address: 1055 N Curtis Rd, Boise, ID 83706

Phone: (208) 367-2121

Website: saintalphonsus.org

Saint Alphonsus Regional Medical Center provides a wide range of medical services, including emergency care, surgery, and specialized treatments. It serves the Boise community with multiple locations for easy access.

3. Visitor Information Centers

Boise Convention & Visitors Bureau

Address: 1101 W Front St #100, Boise, ID 83702

Phone: (208) 344-7777

Website: boise.org

The Boise Convention & Visitors Bureau offers comprehensive visitor information, including maps, guides, and recommendations for attractions, dining, and events in Boise. Visit their downtown office for personalized assistance and local insights.

Idaho State Historical Museum

Address: 610 N Julia Davis Dr, Boise, ID 83702

Phone: (208) 334-2120

Website: history.idaho.gov

Located in Julia Davis Park, the Idaho State Historical Museum not only showcases Idaho's rich history but also serves as a resource center for visitors seeking information on Boise and statewide attractions.

4. Emergency Contacts

Emergency Services (Police, Fire, Medical)

Emergency: 911

Boise Police Department Non-Emergency: (208) 377-6790

Boise Fire Department Non-Emergency: (208) 570-6500

These numbers connect you to emergency services and non-emergency lines for police and fire departments in Boise. Remember to dial 911 for emergencies requiring immediate assistance.

5. Local Organizations and Resources

Boise Metro Chamber of Commerce

Address: 1101 W Front St #100, Boise, ID 83702

Phone: (208) 472-5205

Website: boisechamber.org

The Boise Metro Chamber of Commerce supports local businesses and provides resources for economic development, networking opportunities, and community engagement in Boise.

City of Boise Parks and Recreation

Address: 1104 Royal Blvd, Boise, ID 83706

Phone: (208) 608-7600

Website: cityofboise.org/departments/parks-and-recreation

Boise Parks and Recreation manages and maintains city parks, trails, and recreational facilities. They offer programs and events for residents and visitors to enjoy Boise's outdoor spaces.

6. Educational Institutions

Boise State University

Address: 1910 University Dr, Boise, ID 83725

Phone: (208) 426-1000

Website: boisestate.edu

Boise State University is a leading public research university located in downtown Boise, offering a range of academic programs, cultural events, and athletic activities.

7. Public Libraries

Boise Public Library

Main Branch Address: 715 S Capitol Blvd, Boise, ID 83702

Phone: (208) 972-8200

Website: boisepubliclibrary.org

The Boise Public Library system includes multiple branches throughout the city, providing access to books, digital resources, community programs, and educational workshops.

8. Media Outlets

Idaho Statesman (Newspaper)

Address: 1200 N Curtis Rd, Boise, ID 83706

Phone: (208) 377-6200

Website: idahostatesman.com

The Idaho Statesman is Boise's primary daily newspaper, covering local news, events, and issues affecting the community. It also offers online editions and digital subscriptions.

9. Utilities

Idaho Power

Customer Service: 1-800-488-6151

Website: idahopower.com

Idaho Power provides electricity to residents and businesses in Boise and the surrounding areas. Their website offers account management tools, outage notifications, and energy-saving tips.

10. Tourism Information

Visit Idaho

Website: visitidaho.org

Visit Idaho is the official tourism website for the state, offering information on attractions, outdoor activities, events, and travel resources throughout Idaho, including Boise.

Conclusion

As we conclude this journey through Boise, we hope you've discovered the heart and soul of Idaho's capital city—a place where vibrant culture, outdoor adventure, and community spirit converge to create unforgettable experiences. Whether you've explored the historic landmarks of downtown Boise, hiked the scenic trails of the Boise Foothills, or immersed yourself in the local arts scene, Boise has undoubtedly left an indelible mark on your travels.

Boise's charm lies not only in its picturesque landscapes and thriving urban center but also in the warmth and hospitality of its residents. From the bustling streets of the Basque Block to the tranquil pathways of the Boise River Greenbelt, every corner of this city invites you to uncover its stories, embrace its culture, and connect with its community.

As you reflect on your time in Boise, remember the moments of awe at the Idaho State Capitol, the serenity found in Julia Davis Park, and the flavors savored in Boise's diverse dining scene. Whether you're a visitor planning your next adventure or a local rediscovering your city's treasures, Boise continues to offer endless possibilities for exploration and discovery.

We hope this guide has served as your trusted companion, providing insider tips, detailed recommendations, and practical resources to enhance your Boise experience. As you depart, carry with you the memories of Boise's natural beauty, cultural richness, and the welcoming spirit that defines this remarkable city.

Embrace Boise, where every visit promises new discoveries and cherished memories. Until we meet again in the City of Trees—farewell, and may your travels always lead you back to Boise's embrace.

Printed in Great Britain
by Amazon